# MOVIE CLIPS
*that*
# TEACH & TRAIN

■ by Becky Pike Pluth, M.Ed.

# Dedication

### Brad Pluth
My husband, dreamer, lover, believer chasing the Son,
God's gift to me for life.

### Barb Pike
My mother, my sunshine on cloudy days, my friend, and
role model. Thank you for teaching me to follow through with
commitments and to love the Lord above all else.

**Credits**
Editor: Liz Wheeler
Book Designer/Illustrator: Jody Majeres, Majeres Graphic Design

ISBN 13: 978-0-9794103-2-1
ISBN 10: 0-9794103-2-0

# Contents

# Acknowledgements

Expressing gratitude to those that have come alongside you is such a pleasure. I truly believe it is one of the most enjoyable parts of writing a book. To everyone that made this dream come to life, including my students back in the day at Hopkins that acted as my guinea pigs without knowing, a big thanks.

With the clamoring of cymbals and gongs, I humbly do my best to say thank you to my family and friends. They are the popcorn of my life.

To Liz Wheeler, for not letting me put this idea off one more day and volunteering to help me get this book off the ground. You provided me with endless motivation by pushing me to meet a tight deadline. Your countless hours of research and editing were imperative to this book being on the shelf. Thank you for making all of my articles and this book sound better. We made it!

To Sara Davis, for many phone calls and movie ideas that I wouldn't have remembered myself. Thank you for encouraging me in life and friendship.

Robert Pike (the younger), you inspired me to greater things when you told me that you would help me get this on the web. But, moreover, you talk about the books and ideas to come, believing in my success.

Dan Wheeler, Steve Davis, Rosie Pike, Andrew Pike, Jessica Pike, John Pike, Jesse Mast, Brad Aaberg, Anne Scheuerman and all of my movie experts' memories for movie clips were amazing. You took the time to review my content areas and head me in the right direction…even if your ideas were a bit "off the wall." I am still trying to figure out how kung fu and silent movies made the list. I am so proud to call many of you family.

To Kendra Gruman and Jessica Struck, besides hooking me up with loaner DVDs, you are truly my cheerleaders. You encourage me and show me you believe in me as a friend and a businesswoman.

To Bob Pike, my dad, for taking me to that first National Speakers Association convention and opening my eyes to what would one day be my career. Thank you for believing in my abilities as a teacher and now a trainer.

To my faithful editors, Liz Wheeler, Dr. Sara K. Davis, and Andrea Sisco Pike. Without each of you, my book would have more errors than imaginable. Thank you for turning around pages literally overnight. I know many hours of dedicated hard work went into this, and I am truly thankful.

To Jody Majeres, for your wonderful design inspiration and dedication to this project. When challenges came our way, you found a solution and turned things around. It has been a privilege to work with someone so talented; I am honored to call you my friend.

To Howard McCarley, for believing in my abilities as a trainer from the beginning and giving me the opportunity to grow as a trainer. Together we have tested teaching to every learning style, and this will add to our toolkit. It has been a wonderful journey. Thank you.

To my darling children, Raegan, Broderick, Gabriel and Lucas. Because of you, I have watched many movies I otherwise might not have and have included clips from some of your favorites.

To Kevin Condrin and Ed Schneider, not only did you provide some great ideas for clips, you gave me inspiration and believed in my idea for this book. As soon as your tugboat movie makes it big, I will add it to the list. Hey guys…It's a Mad, Mad, Mad, Mad World!

To my God and Abba Father who has blessed me richly in life and love. To Him be the glory.

# Foreword

Almost every teacher or trainer has, at some point, thought a particular movie scene would make a great learning point in one of his or her programs. Teachers and trainers are odd ducks that way. We look at almost everything around us and find links to what we're trying to help people learn – and that's a good thing!

Over the years, I've used a number of movie clips in a variety of training programs. Why? Because Hollywood has a lot more money to spend on their movies and usually has better actors than we can afford in corporate training videos. When I was doing a program for the Defense Security Institute, I used a clip from *Beverly Hills Cop* where Axel Foley (Eddie Murphy) climbs the fence of a bonded warehouse. When accosted, Axel turns the situation around and soon has everyone opening doors, files, and just about everything else.

While viewing the five-minute clip, the DSI trainers were placed into two groups – one looking for protocols that were violated and the other looking for procedures that were violated. Participants watched with a different focus and the ensuing discussion drove home a variety of learning points much more quickly than any other method I could have chosen.

Over the years, I've tried working with movie production and rental companies to compile the clips onto DVDs that could be sold to teachers and trainers, but could never get the cooperation of the right people to make that project happen.

Becky has gone a step further. Not only do you get the location of clips isolated for you, you also get different content areas to which they might apply to as well as discussion questions you can use to ensure that there is a transfer from simple entertainment value to practical learning points that reinforce your training topics.

She also has done the groundwork on how to use the clips legally. This might seem like a small thing, but it's not. The bigger the corporate pockets, the more likely that using clips without a proper license will cause real financial pain. So let me encourage you to pay close attention on how to obtain a license – and then follow through.

The hundreds of hours of research that she has done will save you not only a lot of time, but a great deal of money. More than that, she is providing a foolproof method of gaining participant involvement in a way that improves retention, application, and transfer. The clips she recommends have been chosen thoughtfully – and so have her recommendations for how to use the clips and handle the discussion to debrief them.

One of the best things is that many of the movies Becky recommends have multiple clips – so purchasing a single video or single video license provides a variety of content. A single investment pays off in multiple ways. She also helps the teacher or trainer avoid the "watch this video" syndrome. All too often we see trainers start a 30- or 60-minute video with no set up or instructions, then leave the room while it's running, and return shortly before the conclusion. Then the first question you hear is, "What did you think?" Most often, the discussion that follows is short and listless. The video has been more a baby sitter or an opportunity for a nap than a dynamic, interactive, memorable, energizing learning experience.

That kind of video use ends with this book! Starting today, you can teach, energize, engage, and inspire your participants. So turn the pages, savor, enjoy, apply, and reap the benefits!

Bob Pike, CSP, CPAE
Founder/Editor, the *Creative Training Techniques* newsletter
Chairman/CEO, The Bob Pike Group

# Introduction

Ten years ago, I taught students about the value of writing down their goals as a junior high and high school teacher. In general, I believe it is important to practice what I preach so I too wrote down my goals. One of my very long-term goals was to write a book. I dared not write down that it would be published as well. At the time, I didn't have a clue that the concept of my book was being birthed there in the classroom.

When I began my teaching career in health science, there were times when I would find a great movie that drove home a specific point. Whether it was on anorexia or dealing with anger, oftentimes a movie said it better than I could. After each movie, I would have discussion questions that would debrief the topic, and I found the discussions did a lot of teaching. My only frustration was that it took two class periods to drive home a point. After a few quarters of watching the whole movie, I began to realize there were certain clips that spoke directly to the topic at hand. It was then that I began to show brief clips to help teach.

After moving from education into corporate training, I continued to show 1- to 4-minute clips throughout trainings. Sometimes I would ask participants in advance to look for certain key lessons; on other occasions, the questions after the clip were the key lesson. I found that participants were really engaged and that we got to the focal point just as quickly as if I had been lecturing and, believe me, it was far more interesting than a lecture. It wasn't until I was researching different forms of media to teach that it became apparent to me that video clips are one of those media forms, and there really weren't any reference resources available.

While I have been using video clips for years, I realized that I always had to remember what clip made a good point or where it was in a movie. Although I knew what movie it was in, I ended up having to re-watch just to find that perfect clip.

I know it takes a lot of energy to be creative in your teaching and training on a regular basis, and I hope this book frees up some of your time so that you may continue coming up with creating other great ideas for teaching and facilitating. One true treasure of this guide is that it saves you trying to remember what movies cover what topic and when. This book will give you many ideas as a starting point. You bring to the table the topic and decide what questions will work for you and your company or school. You may need to adapt some of the questions in order for it to be applied, but this is a starting point.

# How To Use
## *101 Movie Clips that Teach and Train*

Are you teaching or training a key point and want to illustrate it to reinforce information or start a discussion? Simply look to the topical index and find what themes tie into your lesson. The clips in the book are organized by movie title and some clips have multiple themes or "takes" on a topic. Once you have picked your clip, you will find it is broken into three sections: plot summary, scene description and discussion questions. Each film is introduced by topic area. To better help with copyright laws, you will find the movie title, distributor, rating and year released in the next section.

Plot Summary – This will give you an idea of what the entire movie is about. Even if you have never seen the movie, you will be able to get an idea of who the main characters are and the context.

Description of the Scene – Look here to get a brief overview of the clip that is being suggested. Sometimes there is additional background information from the previous scene that will help you understand the context better.

Start Time/End Time – These times will help you cue your clip. Find your clip by setting the counter on your DVD player or VCR to 0:00:00 at the start of the movie. All clips are the exact duration. After reviewing the clip, you may want to shorten or lengthen it based on your points. CAUTION: At times you may see this bold signal. This is a warning that there may be strong language or violence following the scene or a reminder to review the scene for sensitivity to your group. Prior to showing your audience, be sure to review the clip to ensure the material is appropriate for your group.

Duration – This will provide you with the length of the clip so that you can plan your session or lesson. Keep in mind that the focus of these clips is to emphasize the topic and generate discussion rather than have a movie day. In keeping with that methodology, each clip is about 4 minutes or less in duration.

Discussion Questions – The discussion questions focus on a particular theme, but can be varied to spark discussion on a variety of topics. Discussion questions have been designed to take learners from easy-to-answer questions about the clip to application questions. To get the most from your discussions, I have found that starting with questions about the scene is safe. Most people feel comfortable talking about what they just saw. After drawing conclusions from the scene, I have found the most success with having individuals in groups then look at their own work or school situation and apply it to themselves. What will they do differently or the same?

### Avoiding Objections

PREVIEW FIRST! – Although I have done my best to provide clips that are free from obscenities, violence or other questionable content (any exceptions are clearly noted in the Caution! area) there may be a clip that would be offensive to your specific audience and may cause you undue embarrassment or possible human resource issues. Some clips are from PG-13 or R-rated movies but none of the scenes is PG-13 or R-rated. You know your audience best. Armed with that knowledge, preview your selected movie and clip, and be sensitive to your group. The scenes that come before and after may be questionable, so you will want to be sure to cue your scenes precisely. You're the instructor; think before you press play.

The use of a clip in this book does not imply the endorsement of the movie, the actors and their lifestyles, the products used in the movie and so on. The point isn't for me to endorse anything, but merely provide you with a resource to give training and teaching some zip. There are a lot of clips to shop from, but first make sure you are copyright compliant.

### Get Compliant: How to Get Copyright Permission

The question always comes up: do I really need to get permission to use a movie? The answer is YES if you are going to actually show the movie. If you are simply going to verbally describe the scene, then you don't need permission. You may have heard of "fair use" before. This is actually a very narrow copyright rule that allows certain non-profit groups the right to use movies, but it must be for a class that receives credit, among other things. The most ethical route is to purchase a license. To review all copyright laws, visit http://tinyurl.com/i654, or for specifics on fair use and whether your video use would fall under that law, visit http://tinyurl.com/v62y. Licensing can be purchased for one-time use or as an "umbrella" where your company, school, library or church can use movies from authorized titles for a fee.

# Licenses

## Corporate

For companies, there are a variety of license options to choose from based on your specific use. The fee for an Umbrella License® is reasonable and a company can use as many movies as they want internally (not for profit) for one year or a fixed period of time. Motion Picture Licensing Corporation will work with you to customize a license that fits your needs. Because companies vary, there isn't a one-size-fits-all license and MPLC will work with you to get you compliant! All of these licenses can be granted over the phone. For an exact quote and further information, contact MPLC by email at info@mplc.com, by phone at 310.822.8855 or 800.462.8855 or on the Internet at http://www.mplc.com.

## Private Schools

Licensing fees for private schools are based on the student population. For a private school with 200 students, the fee would be about $270 annually. These licenses can be granted over the phone. For an exact quote and further information, contact MPLC by email at info@mplc.com, by phone at 310.822.8855 or 800.462.8855 or on the Internet at http://www.mplc.com.

## Faith-Based Schools and Churches

Licensing fees for churches and faith-based schools are based on the size of congregation or student population. An average congregation attendance of under 500 is about $200 a year; under one thousand would be about $250. For a faith-based school with 200 students, the fee would be about $270. These licenses can be granted over the phone. For an exact quote and further information, contact Christian Video Licensing International by email at info@cvli.org, by phone at 1.888.771.2854 or on the Internet at http://www.cvli.org.

## Public Schools

Licensing fees for public schools are $75 for a one-time viewing license or an annual unlimited Public Performance Site License can be purchased so that schools (kindergarten through twelfth grade) can show movies legally for non-teaching activities. The license can be obtained for an individual school or an entire district. Pricing is based on enrollment for each school or district. Fees start at $300. These licenses can be granted over the phone. For an exact quote and more information, contact Movie Licensing USA by email at mail@movlic.com, by phone at 877.321.1300 or on the Internet at http://www.movlic.com/index.html.

## Public Libraries

A Public Performance Site License for a public library allows an unlimited number of exhibitions of copyrighted entertainment movies for a flat annual fee. The annual license fee is determined by the number of active cardholders the library serves. These licenses can be granted over the phone. For an exact quote and further information, contact MPLC by email at info@mplc.com, by phone at 310.822.8855 or 800.462.8855, or on the internet at http://www.mplc.com or Movie Licensing USA by email at mail@movlic.com, by phone at 888.267.2658 or on the Internet at http://www.movlic.com/index.html.

# 101 MOVIE CLIPS
*that*
## TEACH & TRAIN

# ■ Movie Title:

## *Akeelah and the Bee*

**Distributed By: Lions Gate Films**
**Year Created: 2006**
**MPAA rating: PG**

---

## Plot Summary:

Akeelah Anderson is an intelligent, lovable, yet insecure 11-year-old girl from the South Central District of Los Angeles. Hoping to avoid detention for absences, she participates in her school's first spelling bee and wins, qualifying her for the state competition. Her love of words and her uncanny knack for spelling, along with coaching from Dr. Larabee, drive her to make it to the Scripps National Spelling Bee in Washington, despite her mother's disapproval.

## Description of the Scene:

Tanya, Akeelah's mother, has just gotten to the state regional bee and is furious that Mr. Welch went behind her back to let her daughter participate. Dr. Larabee and Mr. Welch begin to explain that Akeelah had a signed permission slip to attend when Akeelah takes ownership of her actions and admits to forging the signature. Dr. Larabee validates Tanya's feelings, effectively manages the conflict and persuades her to allow Akeelah to compete.

| Topic Area: | Analyzing Issues |
| | Conflict Management |
| | Lying |
| | Negotiation |
| | Ownership |

| Start Time: | **57:00** |
| End Time: | **1:01:00** |
| Clip Duration: | **4:00** |

# Discussion Questions:

- Why did Akeelah forge her father's signature?
- Did Akeelah's taking ownership of the situation play a role in the outcome?
- How did Dr. Larabee diffuse the situation?
- If Dr. Larabee hadn't been there, would the outcome have been the same? Explain.
- How did Tanya negotiate with her daughter?
- How can listening and understanding help us solve a conflict?
- Why is it important to see other points of view?
- Why is it difficult to take responsibility when we feel justified in our actions?
- How can you negotiate a task with peers, a manager, or others on a project?
- How can we be responsible for our own behavior at work and in our projects?

## ■ Movie Title:

# *Akeelah and the Bee*

**Distributed By: Lions Gate Films**
**Year Created: 2006**
**MPAA rating: PG**

---

## Plot Summary:

Akeelah Anderson is an intelligent, lovable, yet insecure 11-year-old girl from the South Central District of Los Angeles. Hoping to avoid detention for absences, she participates in her school's first spelling bee and wins, qualifying her for the state competition. Her love of words and her uncanny knack for spelling, along with coaching from Dr. Larabee, drive her to make it to the Scripps National Spelling Bee in Washington, despite her mother's disapproval.

## Description of the Scene:

Akeelah loses her coach. Akeelah's mother, Tanya, encourages her by saying there are 50,000 other coaches around her in her community.

**Start Time:** **1:12:25**
**End Time:** **1:15:50**
**Clip Duration:** **3:25**

# Discussion Questions:

- Did Akeelah need a coach? Explain.
- How hard was it for Akeelah to find people to coach her?
- What does it take to be a coach? What qualities do they possess?
- How should we choose a coach?
- When is a coach needed?
- Describe a mentor/mentee relationship.
- Think of someone at work that you could offer to coach.

■ # Movie Title:

## *Akeelah and the Bee*

**Distributed By:** **Lions Gate Films**
**Year Created:** **2006**
**MPAA rating:** **PG**

## Plot Summary:

Akeelah Anderson is an intelligent, lovable, yet insecure 11-year-old girl from the South Central District of Los Angeles. Hoping to avoid detention for absences, she participates in her school's first spelling bee and wins, qualifying her for the state competition. Her love of words and her uncanny knack for spelling, along with coaching from Dr. Larabee, drive her to make it to the Scripps National Spelling Bee in Washington, despite her mother's disapproval.

## Description of the Scene:

Akeelah and Dylan are the final two contestants in the Scripps National Spelling Bee. Akeelah knows it's Dylan's last chance to take first place and that his father will be furious if he doesn't win. Akeelah purposely misspells her word, a word she learned from Dylan, so that he can win. Wanting to win fairly, Dylan also purposely misspells the word.

■

**Topic Area:**

Assumptions
Misunderstanding
Problem Solving

Start Time: **1:36:33**
End Time: **1:40:10**
Clip Duration: **3:37**

# Discussion Questions:

- Why would Akeelah purposely throw away a first place win?
- If you were Dylan, what would you have done? Why?
- What assumptions did Akeelah make before purposely misspelling her word?
- Is it easier to take care of our own problems or other people's problems?
- Have you ever seen someone react the way they thought they were supposed to only to realize they misinterpreted the other person? Explain what happened.
- Is it a sign of failure when you try something and it doesn't work?
- How can an individual hurt a team effort?
- What can you do to avoid making assumptions?

# ■ Movie Title:

# *Anger Management*

**Distributed By: Columbia Pictures**
**Year Created: 2003**
**MPAA rating: PG-13**

---

## Plot Summary:

Dave Buznik is a mild-mannered, middle-aged executive assistant awaiting an overdue promotion. However, his non-assertive nature allows others to walk all over him. While aboard a flight, a simple misunderstanding forces Dave into anger management sessions with Dr. Buddy Rydell. Buddy's unconventional methods land Dave in more legal trouble but also give Dave the push needed to stand up for himself.

## Description of the Scene:

Dr. Rydell is busy watching the in-flight movie and pushing Dave to do so. Dave has asked for a set of headphones but can't seem to get anyone to help him. When he does get the flight attendant's attention, a simple misunderstanding lands him in trouble.

■

| Topic Area: | Communication |
| | Conflict Management |
| | Customer Service |
| | Discrimination |
| | Harassment |
| | Negotiation |

| Start Time: | **05:30** |
| End Time: | **08:10** |
| Clip Duration: | **2:40** |

■ —————————————————————————

# Discussion Questions:

- Was Dave harassing the "stewardess" or the in-flight security officer? If so, what did he do?
- Could the parties involved in this scene have communicated better? If so, how?
- What impact did the flight attendant's customer service have on the situation?
- Whose responsibility is a harassment-free workplace?
- What are the most important aspects of good customer service?
- What can you do to provide the best service possible to your customers?

# ■ Movie Title:

## *Apollo 13*

**Distributed By:** MCA/Universal Pictures
**Year Created:** 1995
**MPAA rating:** PG

---

## Plot Summary:

Based on the true story of the thirteenth Apollo mission in 1970, the crew of astronauts head to space on a "routine" flight to the moon. A situation occurs, and the prospect of returning to earth begins to fade. Mission Control struggles to find creative solutions to avert tragedy and get its astronauts home.

## Description of the Scene:

Jim Lovell, an astronaut, is interviewed on TV when he reminisces about his fighter plane's failure and the resources he needed to land on his aircraft carrier safely. Without warning, his instruments shorted out leaving him in the "dark." What seemed to be a tragedy turned out to save his life because the darkness allowed him to see and follow the ship's wake.

|              | Distractions    |
| Topic Area:  | Focus           |
|              | Irony           |
|              | Problem Solving |

Start Time: **1:45:00**
End Time: **1:46:33**
Clip Duration: **1:33**

---

# Discussion Questions:

- What did it take for Jim to "see" his landing goal?
- Was it his original plan? Did it matter? Why or why not?
- Describe a time when Plan B turned out better than Plan A.
- Have you ever been a part of a project where the focus was strictly on one solution? What happened?
- Why is flexibility an essential part of any team?
- What happens when you become distracted and miss something important?
- What at work distracts you from solution-oriented thinking?
- What can you do to see beyond the first or obvious solution?
- How do distractions hinder/help your performance?

## ■ Movie Title:

# *Austin Powers: International Man of Mystery*

**Distributed By:** New Line Cinema
**Year Created:** 1997
**MPAA rating:** PG-13

---

## Plot Summary:

After 30 years of being frozen, British secret agent Austin Powers is brought back to life to foil Dr. Evil's plans to hold the world hostage with a nuclear bomb for a ransom of $100 billion. Austin Powers and his partner Vanessa Kensington join forces to stop him.

## Description of the Scene:

Dr. Evil's son, Scott, tries to give him some advice. Each time Scott tries to talk, Dr. Evil stops him by saying, "Shhh." After several attempts, a completely frustrated Scott gives up.

| | |
|---|---|
| **Topic Area:** | Communication |
| | Listening |

| | |
|---|---|
| **Start Time:** | **1:05:45** |
| **End Time:** | **1:06:15** |
| **Clip Duration:** | **0:30** |

■ ───────────────────────────────

# Discussion Questions:

- Is there anything Scott could have done to make Dr. Evil listen? If so, what?
- Share about a time when a superior wouldn't listen to you.
- What does listening have to do with communication?
- Is there a difference between listening and hearing? Explain.
- How does poor listening lead to problems?
- How do you feel when a co-worker or peer doesn't listen to you?
- What can you do to be a better listener?
- What can you do to get those above you to hear you and your ideas?

# ■ Movie Title:

## *Austin Powers: The Spy Who Shagged Me*

**Distributed By:** **New Line Cinema**
**Year Created:** **1999**
**MPAA rating:** **PG-13**

---

## Plot Summary:

Dr. Evil travels back in time to steal Austin Powers' "mojo." Austin, accompanied by Felicity Shagwell, must travel back in time to recover his vitality. Meanwhile, Dr. Evil clones a mini-me of himself, falls in love, works on his relationship with his son and continues his plot to take over the world, again, this time with a gigantic "laser."

## Description of the Scene:

Dr. Evil's co-conspirator, Mustafa, is at the bottom of a ravine injured. He is calling out to his adversary, Austin Powers, for help but Austin ignores his pleas, leaving him to suffer.

| Topic Area: | Ethics |
|---|---|
| | Helping Others |

| | |
|---|---|
| Start Time: | **34:15** |
| End Time: | **34:45** |
| Clip Duration: | **0:30** |

## Discussion Questions:

- What happened in this scene?
- Was it wrong of Austin to leave Mustafa injured and not help him? Was it ethical?
- Do different situations call for different responses? Explain.
- How do you determine what is or isn't ethical at work?
- Have you worked on a project with someone from another team who felt like an adversary? What happened?
- How hard is it to help someone you don't care for?
- What can you do to help others at work, even when you don't want to?

## ■ Movie Title:

# *Behind Enemy Lines*

Distributed By: **20th Century Fox**
Year Created: **2001**
MPAA rating: **PG-13**

---

## Plot Summary:

Sick of all the recon missions, Chris Burnett flies slightly off-course to check out an interesting target over Bosnia. He soon finds himself alone, attempting to outrun an army and hoping that Admiral Reigart can get him out alive.

## Description of the Scene:

Admiral Reigart asks Burnett why he's leaving the Navy with all of his potential. Burnett says he is sick of all the "practice" missions. The Admiral talks about how practice is preparation for war.

**Topic Area:**          Perseverance
                              Quitting

| | |
|---|---|
| **Start Time:** | **9:30** |
| **End Time:** | **12:15** |
| **Clip Duration:** | **2:45** |

---

# Discussion Questions:

- Why is Burnett leaving the Navy?
- Does Burnett's reason say anything about him and his job? If so, what?
- Is Burnett quitting? Why or why not?
- Why is he tired of preparing?
- When is it most difficult to persevere at work?
- Is it ever appropriate to quit? Explain.
- What can you do to overcome challenging times at work?
- What can you do to help others make it over the hurdles that build up at work?
- What are some methods of preparing? How can you integrate them at work?

■ # Movie Title:

## *Big*

**Distributed By:** 20th Century Fox
**Year Created:** 1988
**MPAA rating:** PG

---

## Plot Summary:

When you're a 12-year-old who wants to make decisions for himself but can't, what do you wish for? To be BIG! Josh Baskin did just that and found his wish came true, and now he must learn to be a 30-year-old.

## Description of the Scene:

Josh is in a meeting and is "playing" with a toy robot but doesn't understand what makes it a fun toy. Paul rattles off marketing statistics, but Josh still doesn't get why it's supposed to be fun. Josh brainstorms a different toy idea that would be fun.

■

| Topic Area: | Impressions |
| | Innovative Thinking |
| | Marketing |

| | |
|---|---|
| **Start Time:** | **42:30** |
| **End Time:** | **45:15** |
| **Clip Duration:** | **2:45** |

---

# Discussion Questions:

- Why does Paul give stats in response to Josh's question?
- Should Paul have been able to clearly articulate an answer to Josh's question?
- How could Paul have encouraged Josh to come up with an answer to his own question?
- Can marketing impact people's perspective positively? Negatively?
- Describe a company that has successful marketing. What have they done to create/maintain that image?
- Identify someone who is highly creative and ask for feedback on how to become more creative and innovative.

## ■ Movie Title:

# *Bobby Jones: Stroke of Genius*

**Distributed By: Columbia Tristar Home Entertainment**
**Year Created: 2004**
**MPAA rating: PG**

---

## Plot Summary:

In 1930, the world would see Bobby Jones, an amateur golfer, win all four of golf's major tournaments, a feat unequaled to this day. Determined to master the game, he is faced with overcoming health problems, family tensions and his temper. Jones' style modeled integrity, passion and a love for the game that inspired the world.

## Description of the Scene:

In the final round of the U.S. Open tournament, Bobby Jones (paired with Walter Hagan) is setting up for his shot and causes his ball to move. He sees the ball move, but no one else does. The official leaves the decision up to Bobby whether to continue the round with or without a penalty.

| Topic Area: | Accountability |
| | Analyzing Issues |
| | Honesty |
| | Integrity |
| | Values |

Start Time: **1:18:55**
End Time: **1:21:00**
Clip Duration: **2:05**

## Discussion Questions:

- Why did Bobby take the penalty?
- What impression did his decision leave on those around him?
- Which would feel better: taking the penalty and winning? Or skipping the penalty and winning? Why?
- If you were given the option to not take a penalty, would you? Why?
- How do you analyze issues and make decisions?
- What can you do to better analyze a task or situation?
- When in a sticky situation, what steps can you take to ensure you make a decision that is right even if it's not the easy way out?
- Is integrity a moment-by-moment decision or an overarching value? Explain.
- What process can you put in place to hold yourself accountable at work?

# ■ Movie Title:

## *Cars*

**Distributed By: Walt Disney**
**Year Created: 2006**
**MPAA rating: G**

---

## Plot Summary:

Lightning McQueen is a rookie know-it-all race car that fires his third crew chief of the season and decides he can do it on his own. While showing off, he winds up tying instead of winning and now he and Chick Hicks and The King go head-to-head to determine who will be the next Piston Cup champion. On his way to the race-off at the Los Angeles Speedway, Lightning lands himself in the Radiator Springs jail where he learns about respect and picks up a few racing tricks as well.

## Description of the Scene:

Lightning is on the final laps of the race. He's showing off by not pitting with the rest of the cars. He ends, barely tying the race. He assumes he has won and talks about how he didn't need anyone else to do it.

| Topic Area: | Failure |
| | Making Mistakes |
| | Teamwork |

| | |
| --- | --- |
| Start Time: | **7:00** |
| End Time: | **10:21** |
| Clip Duration: | **3:21** |

---

# Discussion Questions:

- Why did Lightning almost lose the race?
- What was his pit crew's reaction?
- Was it a sign of failure on Lightning's part to try something new by not pitting? If not, what was the real problem?
- What traits describe a productive and enjoyable team player?
- What is failure?
- Can we learn from our failures? Explain.
- What is the most difficult part of working on a team?
- How does cooperation help solve problems?
- What can an individual contribute to the success of the whole?
- What can you do to ensure you learn from a mistake or failure?

# ■ Movie Title:

## *Cars*

**Distributed By: Walt Disney**
**Year Created: 2006**
**MPAA rating: G**

---

## Plot Summary:

Lightning McQueen is a rookie know-it-all race car that fires his third crew chief of the season and decides he can do it on his own. While showing off, he winds up tying instead of winning and now he and Chick Hicks and The King go head-to-head to determine who will be the next Piston Cup champion. On his way to the race-off at the Los Angeles Speedway, Lightning lands himself in the Radiator Springs jail where he learns about respect and picks up a few racing tricks as well.

## Description of the Scene:

Lightning, Chick Hicks and The King are competing in a race-off for the Piston Cup. It's The King's final race and the rookie's first chance at a big win; the pressure is on. As Lightning is about to finish in first place, he notices that Chick Hicks has forced The King off the track. Just before the finish line, Lightning screeches to a halt and heads back to push The King across the finish line, allowing Chick Hicks to pass him and win.

■

| Topic Area: | Cheating |
| | Decision Making |
| | Helping Others |
| | Teamwork |
| | Winning |

Start Time: **1:39:33**
End Time: **1:43:41**
Clip Duration: **4:08**

# Discussion Questions:

- Why did Lightning make the choice to go back? Was it worth losing a big race over? Explain.
- Why did Lightning win?
- What influence might Lightning's decision have on others?
- Describe a situation where someone indicated they cared more about immediate gratification versus long-term results.
- In what ways do you control your life?
- In what ways do others influence your life?
- Who has the most influence on the things you do on a daily basis?
- When a decision has risk associated with it, what can you do to make the best decision?

# ■ Movie Title:

## *Cast Away*

**Distributed By:** **20th Century Fox, Dreamworks**
**Year Created:** **2000**
**MPAA rating:** **PG-13**

## Plot Summary:

Life for Chuck Noland, a FedEx manager, is systematic and precise. He sets high standards for his team and is passionate about punctuality. After exchanging gifts on Christmas Eve with his girlfriend, almost-fiancé Kelly, he boards a plane that is caught in a storm and crashes into the Pacific. As the sole survivor, he washes up on an island where his new passion is survival. Four years later, he attempts to find a way home to an already-married Kelly.

## Description of the Scene:

Stranded on the island, Chuck discovers coconuts and attempts to open them to access the milk inside. First he struggles, but, through trial and error, eventually perfects the approach.

| Topic Area: | Improvements |
|---|---|
| | Perseverance |
| | Trial and Error |

| | |
|---|---|
| Start Time: | **39:38** |
| End Time: | **42:25** |
| Clip Duration: | **2:47** |

# Discussion Questions:

- What is Chuck's goal with the coconut?
- Did Chuck have the tools and knowledge to be successful? Explain.
- How many attempts did it take for Chuck to be successful?
- What did Chuck need to do differently to reach his goal?
- Chuck had to "think outside the box" to find a solution. How can you practice "thinking outside the box" in a specific situation at work?
- Share a time when you felt frustrated and wanted to give up.
- What are the benefits and drawbacks to persevering?
- What happens if we quit trying before we have found the best solution?
- How can we apply persistence at work?

# ■ Movie Title:

## *Cast Away*

**Distributed By:** **20th Century Fox, Dreamworks**
**Year Created:** **2000**
**MPAA rating:** **PG-13**

---

## Plot Summary:

Life for Chuck Noland, a FedEx manager, is systematic and precise. He sets high standards for his team and is passionate about punctuality. After exchanging gifts on Christmas Eve with his girlfriend, almost-fiancé Kelly, he boards a delivery plane which ultimately gets caught in a storm and crashes into the Pacific. As the sole survivor, he washes up on an island where his new passion is survival. Four years later, he attempts to find a way home to an already-married Kelly.

## Description of the Scene:

Chuck is stranded on the island after the crash. He collects all the FedEx packages that washed ashore and opens them. He opens a volleyball, a dress with netting fringe which he then uses for a fish net, an ice skate he creatively uses as an ax and the list goes on. However, there is one package with a painted angel wing on it he decides not to open.

■

Creativity
Problem Solving

Start Time: **1:01:36**
End Time: **1:05:00**
Clip Duration: **3:14**

---

# Discussion Questions:

- He doesn't open up a box with the painted angel wing. Why? What would you do?
- What were creative uses for some of the things he opened?
- Can creativity be learned? If so, how?
- Share a time when you had to think "outside the box."
- When faced with a problem, what specific steps do you take to solve it?
- How can being creative help you in your job?
- The next time you have a problem, how will you use creativity to help solve it?
- Do you tend to be a methodical or trial-and-error problem-solver? What are the benefits and drawbacks of each approach?

## ■ Movie Title:

## *Changing Lanes*

**Distributed By:** **Paramount Pictures**
**Year Created:** **2002**
**MPAA rating:** **R**

## Plot Summary:

A Wall Street lawyer rushes to file legal papers involving a multi-million dollar trust when he is involved in a car accident. While the attorney is discussing the accident with the drunken salesman who collided with him, he unknowingly drops the papers and heads to court. Once there, he realizes he doesn't have them, and the hunt begins. While searching for the file, he questions the moral and ethical actions of his law firm.

## Description of the Scene:

Gavin, a Wall Street attorney, discusses his plans with a senior partner. Aware that Gavin's conscience is interfering with the case, he tries to convince Gavin that what the law firm does is in the best interest of everyone.

**Topic Area:**

Courage
Critical Thinking
Ethics
Integrity
Sales

**Start Time:** 1:23:25
**End Time:** 1:24:12
**Clip Duration:** 0:47

# Discussion Questions:

- Are Gavin's convictions justified? Why or why not?
- How are his convictions getting in the way of doing his job? Does it matter?
- Does it matter that Mr. Dunne was manipulated into signing the papers or is that just part of sales?
- What is the ethical thing to do in this situation?
- Who decides what is or isn't ethical?
- What is the difference between persuasion and manipulation?
- When an ethical dilemma occurs at work or school, what do you do? Why?
- What can you do to guard yourself against unethical or dishonest situations?

## ■ Movie Title:

## *Chariots of Fire*

**Distributed By: Warner Brothers**
**Year Created: 1981**
**MPAA rating: PG**

---

## Plot Summary:

This film is based on the true story of two British track athletes competing in the 1924 Summer Olympics. Eric Liddell is a Christian who runs for God, and Harold Abrahams is a Jew who competes to prove his place in society. Both experience struggles but come out winners not only in the Olympics but in life.

## Description of the Scene:

Eric has been told his race will be held on Sunday. Because of his faith, he refuses to run because it is the Sabbath. The Olympic committee and others are putting pressure on him to race anyway. Eric stands up for what he believes in and pushes back.

| Topic Area: | Beliefs |
| | Ethics |
| | Peer Pressure |
| | Values |

| | |
| --- | --- |
| Start Time: | **1:27:15** |
| End Time: | **1:30:15** |
| Clip Duration: | **3:00** |

---

# Discussion Questions:

- Is Eric's reasoning out of line? Explain.
- Did the Olympic committee and others have the right to push Eric to go against his beliefs and values? Why or why not?
- What would you have done if you were Eric and you were asked to go against your beliefs or values for your job, friends, etc?
- How does peer pressure and others' opinions affect your decisions?
- What can you do to be proactive versus reactive in a situation that involves beliefs and values in the workplace?

## ■ Movie Title:

# The Chronicles of Narnia:
# The Lion, the Witch and the Wardrobe

**Distributed By:** Walt Disney
**Year Created:** 2005
**MPAA rating:** PG

---

## Plot Summary:

Sent away from London during World War II, Peter, Edmund, Susan and Lucy head to the home of an eccentric professor. One day, during a game of hide-and-seek, Lucy hides in the wardrobe and finds the magical land of Narnia where animals talk and are ruled by the beloved Aslan. Lucy learns that Narnia is currently under the control of the White Witch, Jadis, and only Lucy and her siblings can defeat the witch.

## Description of the Scene:

Peter tells the General and Edmund that Aslan is dead and that it is time to go home. Edmund urges Peter to lead them into battle and gives him positive feedback and support. Peter goes from not believing in himself to having faith that it can be done.

| Topic Area: | Feedback |
| | Leadership |
| | Motivation |

Start Time: **1:46:15**
End Time: **1:47:15**
Clip Duration: **1:00**

---

# Discussion Questions:

- Why did Peter want to just give up and go home?
- Why does Peter change his mind?
- How did Edmund inspire Peter to be their leader?
- What does it take to inspire others? Explain.
- What is leadership?
- Can anyone be a leader? If so, how?
- Who can you give positive feedback to this week?
- What can you do to take on more of a leadership role at work?

## ■ Movie Title:

# *The Chronicles of Narnia: The Lion, the Witch and the Wardrobe*

**Distributed By:** **Walt Disney**
**Year Created:** **2005**
**MPAA rating:** **PG**

---

## Plot Summary:

Sent away from London during World War II, Peter, Edmund, Susan and Lucy head to the home of an eccentric professor. One day, during a game of hide-and-seek, Lucy hides in the wardrobe and finds the magical land of Narnia where animals talk and are ruled by the beloved Aslan. Lucy learns that Narnia is currently under the control of the White Witch, Jadis, and only Lucy and her siblings can defeat the witch.

## Description of the Scene:

Lucy, Susan and Peter are being led by Mr. and Mrs. Beaver to Aslan and are trying to cross the river before it melts. With slabs of ice breaking away, they begin to cross over until the White Witch's wolves have them surrounded. With Mr. Beaver telling Peter to kill the wolf and Susan wanting him to surrender, Peter finds a creative solution to his problem.

| Topic Area: | Creativity |
| | Decision Making |
| | Peer Pressure |
| | Problem Solving |

| Start Time: | **1:13:00** |
| End Time: | **1:15:30** |
| Clip Duration: | **2:30** |

# Discussion Questions:

- How did Peter respond to the conflicting messages from Mr. Beaver and Susan?
- Peter, amidst chaos, found a creative solution. Was this solution better than Susan or Mr. Beaver's? Explain.
- When there are multiple options, how do you determine the best solution?
- When under pressure, is it difficult to make decisions? Explain.
- When up against a tight timeline, what can you do to creatively solve problems?
- What can you do to practice thinking more creatively?

## ■ Movie Title:

# *Dead Man Walking*

**Distributed By: Gramercy Pictures**
**Year Created: 1995**
**MPAA rating: R**

---

## Plot Summary:

Matthew Poncelet is a convicted murderer on Death Row and is desperate for help to avoid execution. He sends a letter to a caring nun, Sister Prejean, who shows sympathy for him and his victims and their families. Sister Prejean battles the paradox of caring for a condemned man while understanding the heinousness of his crimes. In addition to her temporal help, the nun also tries to reach out to him spiritually.

## Description of the Scene:

Sister Prejean is talking with Matthew at the prison. In this particular meeting, she addresses his racist comments and general prejudice. Poncelet denies being prejudiced. Sister then points out different types of prejudice and tries to help him see it is wrong.

| Topic Area: | Prejudice |
| --- | --- |
| | Racism |
| | Stereotypes |

| | |
| --- | --- |
| **Start Time:** | **42:00** |
| **End Time:** | **43:45** |
| **Clip Duration:** | **1:45** |

# Discussion Questions:

- What did Matthew say that reflected prejudice?
- What examples did Sister Prejean give of his remarks?
- Where did Matthew's prejudice come from?
- What prejudice did Sister bring up that others could have toward Matthew, a convicted murderer?
- How does a person's outward appearance impact what we think about him/her?
- What is the difference between prejudice and racism?
- Have you ever been pre-judged by someone based on a stereotype? How did you feel?
- What can you do to not judge others based on looks or past actions?

## ■ Movie Title:

# *Dead Poet's Society*

**Distributed By: Touchstone Pictures**
**Year Created: 1989**
**MPAA rating: PG**

---

## Plot Summary:

Shy Todd Anderson and popular Neil Perry are roommates at an upscale college prep school. The two are inspired by the English teacher, Professor Keating, who encourages them to go against the status quo.

## Description of the Scene:

Professor Keating is passionately teaching his students to embrace each moment and seize the day. He reminds them that life is short by sharing photos of previous graduates who are no longer alive to inspire the students to *carpe diem*.

| Topic Area: | Coaching |
| | Driving for Results |
| | Learning Styles |
| | Motivation |

| Start Time: | **13:45** |
| End Time: | **16:30** |
| Clip Duration: | **2:45** |

# Discussion Questions:

- Why does Professor Keating show pictures of students who died?
- What impact did the visual have on the lesson?
- What did Keating do to demonstrate his passion?
- Professor Keating is a teacher; is he also a coach? Why or why not?
- How did Keating's lesson appeal to multiple learning styles?
- How can you be a coach although you may not have the title?
- What do you do to push yourself and drive for the best results possible?
- What can you do in your next meeting to meet different learning styles?
- Describe the qualities of your best coach. What qualities can you begin to emulate?

■ **Movie Title:**

# *Dead Poet's Society*

Distributed By: **Touchstone Pictures**
Year Created: **1989**
MPAA rating: **PG**

---

## Plot Summary:

Shy Todd Anderson and popular Neil Perry are roommates at an upscale college prep school. The two are inspired by the English teacher, Professor Keating, who encourages them to go against the status quo.

## Description of the Scene:

Professor Keating jumps up on a desk and begins to talk about perspective. He encourages his class to do the same, challenging them to look at things with a different set of eyes.

Analyzing Issues
Learning Styles
Perspective

| | |
|---|---|
| Start Time: | **43:00** |
| End Time: | **44:15** |
| Clip Duration: | **1:15** |

# Discussion Questions:

- Why does Professor Keating get on his desk?
- How would standing on a desk help teach his lesson?
- What makes something memorable or easy to remember?
- Is there value in seeing things from a different perspective or through someone else's eyes?
- Have you ever changed your mind about an issue after gaining a new perspective?
- Can perspective impact how we analyze issues? Explain.
- How can you learn to look at things from a different perspective?

## ■ Movie Title:

# *Dumb and Dumber*

**Distributed By:** **New Line Cinema**
**Year Created:** **1994**
**MPAA rating:** **PG-13**

---

## Plot Summary:

Best friends Lloyd and Harry are well-meaning but truly brainless.
Jobless, Lloyd and Harry find a suitcase full of money that belongs to
the lovely Mary. They decide to get it back to her, but in the process,
encounter one accident and misfortune after another. They travel to
Aspen, Colorado, and become mixed up in a kidnapping but remain
clueless as to what they are now part of.

## Description of the Scene:

Mary starts a playful snowball fight with Harry, and he goes ballistic.

■

Conflict Management
Courage

Start Time: **1:17:45**
End Time: **1:18:45**
Clip Duration: **1:00**

# Discussion Questions:

- What began in fun ended up in a "deadly" fight. Why?
- As Harry began to get more upset with the situation, could he have done things differently? If so, what?
- What questions could Harry have asked to quickly resolve the conflict?
- Have you ever been on a project where a small issue ends up "snowballing" into something bigger? What happened? What could have been done sooner to resolve things?
- Are there people at work you tend to lock horns with? What causes the conflict?
- Why is it difficult to stand up for what you believe and be a bigger person amidst conflict?
- Can conflict be prevented? If so, how?
- What can you do to resolve conflict on the job?

## Movie Title:

# *Edward Scissorhands*

**Distributed By:** **20<sup>th</sup> Century Fox**
**Year Created:** **1990**
**MPAA rating:** **PG-13**

---

## Plot Summary:

Peg Bogs finishes her day selling Avon products and decides to stop at the large empty mansion only to find Edward, an artificial man, who has scissors for hands. Edward was created by a kind inventor who didn't have the chance to finish his final project. Peg brings Edward back into town where he tries to fit in, learn a trade and learn about life.

## Description of the Scene:

Peg's husband quizzes Edward about what he would do if he found a briefcase full of money. Edward, with his child-like thinking, declares that he would buy nice things for all his friends. This is seen as immoral and unethical by Peg's husband who tells Edward he should bring it to the police. Edward tries to understand that the nice thing is not always the right thing.

| Topic Area: | Accountability |
| | Ethics |
| | Integrity |
| | Trust |

**Start Time:** **1:11:45**
**End Time:** **1:13:30**
**Clip Duration:** **1:45**

---

# Discussion Questions:

- Regarding the briefcase dilemma, who is right? Edward or Peg's husband? Why?
- Why is it important to have integrity in any situation?
- How much influence do peers and co-workers have on your behavior?
- Is honesty always rewarded in the short-run? In the long-run? Explain.
- Is spending time surfing the internet, talking with co-workers, playing games, checking credit card statements, planning trips etc. ethical to do while at work? Why or why not?
- What can you do to manage yourself and your time wisely at work?

# ■ Movie Title:

# *Emma*

**Distributed By:** **Buena Vista**
**Year Created:** **1996**
**MPAA rating:** **PG**

---

## Plot Summary:

A romantic comedy based on Jane Austen's book of the same name, the young Englishwoman, Emma, is the town's matchmaker. She encounters complications when attempting to set up her dear friend Harriet. A simple task becomes a big problem as a chain of misunderstandings unravel. Throughout it all, Emma learns that she too has a true love, but her meddling may have ruined her chances to be with him.

## Description of the Scene:

Mr. Knightley confronts Emma about insulting and demoralizing the old Miss Bates. Emma plays down the situation, but Mr. Knightley is determined to make her see that she is wrong.

■

Confrontation
Feedback

# Discussion Questions:

- What worked with how Mr. Knightley handled confrontation with Emma?
- If feedback is given constructively, can it still be taken negatively? Why or why not?
- What was the result of Mr. Knightley giving Emma constructive feedback?
- Did Emma hear the feedback? Why?
- What should the next step be after giving feedback?
- When should confrontation happen?
- Have you ever given feedback to someone? What happened? What worked?
- Think of a time when you received feedback. What went well? What went poorly?
- What can you do to better receive and proactively give feedback at work?

# Movie Title:

## *The Empire Strikes Back*

**Distributed By:** 20<sup>th</sup> **Century Fox**
**Year Created:** **1980**
**MPAA rating:** **PG**

---

## Plot Summary:

The "Star Wars" saga continues as Han Solo, Princess Leia and Chewbacca battle to save the galaxy from Darth Vader and the Imperial army. Meanwhile, Luke Skywalker seeks to learn the secrets of the Jedi from the ancient Yoda—lessons Luke will need to master before facing Darth Vader.

## Description of the Scene:

Luke feels defeated because he believes his sunken X-wing fighter plane will never be recovered from the swamp. Yoda shares that one's physical size has nothing to do with the ability to raise the fighter. Luke declares the challenge is just too big.

| | |
|---|---|
| **Topic Area:** | Belief |
| | Faith |
| | Perseverance |

| | |
|---|---|
| **Start Time:** | **1:08:15** |
| **End Time:** | **1:10:00** |
| **Clip Duration:** | **1:45** |

■ _____

# Discussion Questions:

- Why isn't Luke able to accomplish this task?
- Have you ever been assigned a task where you felt like Luke? Explain.
- Do actions speak louder than words? If so, why?
- Have you ever worked with someone that persevered even through the toughest challenges? What impact did their attitude have on others?
- How does it feel to be given a huge project to do on your own? What does it take to start the task?
- The next time an "impossible" task comes your way, how can you make it manageable?
- What role does faith in your abilities play in your successful completion of a project?
- If you lack faith in yourself, what can you do to increase your self-confidence?

# ■ Movie Title:

## *Employee of the Month*

**Distributed By:** **Lions Gate Films**
**Year Created:** **2006**
**MPAA rating:** **PG-13**

---

## Plot Summary:

Zack, a slacker box boy, works at Super Club, lives with his grandma, and is basically just getting by. The manager announces that Vince has won the "Employee of the Month" award for 17 months straight. Coincidentally, the gorgeous new hire, Amy, is said to only date "Employee of the Month" winners. Although Zack could care less about the award, he competes to earn employee of the month to gain Amy's attention.

## Description of the Scene:

Zack is on duty and decides to deface Vince's employee of the month picture. After doing that, he skates off, slashing a product for a kid so he'll get a price break. Zack then puts the marker on Semi to avoid being blamed for the defacing.

■

| Topic Area: | Ethics |
| --- | --- |
| | Human Resource Issues |
| | Principles |
| | Safety |

| Start Time: | **01:20** |
| --- | --- |
| End Time: | **02:35** |
| Clip Duration: | **1:15** |

# Discussion Questions:

- What unethical behaviors did Zack exhibit?
- Is there anything wrong with Zack's practical joke? Explain.
- Is Zack contributing to the company? Does it matter if he doesn't?
- What, if any, human resource violations are in this scene?
- What safety issues are in this scene?
- What problems can occur when policies and procedures aren't followed?
- What kind of effort should we put into our job?
- What are some of our most critical policies?
- How can you solve a conflict without resorting to anger?
- Does this scene portray Zack's behavior as endearing and fun or unethical? Explain what impact that perspective has on viewers.

## ■ Movie Title:

# *A Few Good Men*

**Distributed By:** **Columbia Pictures**
**Year Created:** **1992**
**MPAA rating:** **R**

---

## Plot Summary:

Lieutenant Daniel Kaffee, a Navy lawyer who has never been to trial and plea bargains most cases, defends two Marines accused of murdering another Marine. The defense is originally based on the premise that a "code red" was ordered, but the only proof the defense has is the testimony of the convicted. While interviewing Colonel Jessup, the team realizes something isn't lining up and the dramatic courtroom thriller begins.

## Description of the Scene:

CAUTION! **Language right before clip.**

Kaffee is coaching his Navy softball league when another attorney arrives, visibly angry that Kaffee blew off their meeting. In the space of a minute, Kaffee is able to successfully plea bargain by accurately manipulating the facts in his favor.

Start Time: **08:30**

End Time: **09:37**

Clip Duration: **1:07**

# Discussion Questions:

- Was Kaffee successful in his plea bargain? Explain.
- What did Kaffee do while negotiating? Was this in his favor?
- What problem did Kaffee identify that made the other lawyer view it as his problem too?
- Who do you know to be a skilled negotiator? What have you observed that makes them skilled?
- Does knowing the individual with whom you will be negotiating matter? Explain.
- What difficulties do you have in negotiating? What impact does that have on your success in negotiating?
- How can you prepare for a negotiation?
- What can you do to become a better negotiator?

# Movie Title:

## *Finding Forrester*

**Distributed By: Columbia Pictures**
**Year Created: 2000**
**MPAA rating: PG-13**

---

## Plot Summary:

Jamal Wallace is an incredibly talented and intelligent basketball player who receives a scholarship to a prep school in Manhattan. He befriends the introverted author William Forrester who becomes his mentor. Their friendship helps William overcome his hermit-like existence and Jamal overcome racial prejudices to pursue his dream of writing.

## Description of the Scene:

Jamal watches as Massie, Forrester's delivery man, pulls up in his BMW to deliver groceries to Forrester. He walks over to his car and stands there watching as Massie desperately tries to lock the car. Jamal asks why he's so worried; after all, it's just a car. Massie says it's not just a car and if Jamal knew anything about BMWs, he would know that. Jamal breaks down Massie's assumptions, discriminations and stereotypes as he spouts off facts that not even Massie knew about BMW.

| Topic Area: | Assumptions |
| | Discrimination |
| | Stereotypes |

| | |
|---|---|
| Start Time: | **17:40** |
| End Time: | **19:45** |
| Clip Duration: | **2:05** |

# Discussion Questions:

- What assumptions did Massie, Forrester's delivery man, have?
- Is Massie discriminating against Jamal? Explain.
- Did Massie's reaction to Jamal reflect on the neighborhood? On Jamal's race?
- Why are assumptions made in certain neighborhoods?
- What types of assumptions are made at work?
- What is discrimination? Who does it affect?
- Is racial stereotyping harmful to society? Explain.
- What information should we use about people when deciding what they are capable of accomplishing?
- What role should race, creed, weight, sex, etc. have in deciding what tasks someone is able to do?
- What can you do to eliminate discrimination, stereotyping and erroneous assumptions about those you work with?

■ # Movie Title:

## *Finding Forrester*

**Distributed By:** **Columbia Pictures**
**Year Created:** **2000**
**MPAA rating:** **PG-13**

---

## Plot Summary:

Jamal Wallace is an incredibly talented and intelligent basketball player who receives a scholarship to a prep school in Manhattan. He befriends the introverted author William Forrester who becomes his mentor. Their friendship helps William overcome his hermit-like existence and Jamal overcome racial prejudices to pursue his dream of writing.

## Description of the Scene:

**CAUTION! Begin and end exactly on the timer; there is footage on either end of the clip that might be offensive.**

Jamal learns a lesson from Forrester on the importance of asking questions and collecting data. Forrester challenges Jamal's reasoning behind collecting data and information that doesn't pertain to Jamal.

Communication
Data Gathering

Start Time: **35:29**
End Time: **36:49**
Clip Duration: **1:20**

# Discussion Questions:

- What does this scene tell us about communication? Data gathering?
- Do you agree with Forrester's reasons behind his questions? Explain.
- What is the importance of questions in data gathering?
- Why is communication important when working in a group?
- What role does data gathering play in your job?
- Do you spend enough time on analysis prior to starting a project? Explain.
- What happens when the wrong questions are asked in the analysis phase of a task, job or program?
- How can you ensure that you are asking the right questions to get the right information?

# ■ Movie Title:

## *Finding Forrester*

**Distributed By: Columbia Pictures**
**Year Created: 2000**
**MPAA rating: PG-13**

---

## Plot Summary:

Jamal Wallace is an incredibly talented and intelligent basketball player who receives a scholarship to a prep school in Manhattan. He befriends the introverted author William Forrester who becomes his mentor. Their friendship helps William overcome his hermit-like existence and Jamal overcome racial prejudices to pursue his dream of writing.

## Description of the Scene:

Professor Crawford accuses Jamal Wallace of cheating.

| Topic Area: | Accusations |
| --- | --- |
| | Assumptions |
| | Discrimination |
| | Stereotypes |

Start Time: **1:15:19**
End Time: **1:16:06**
Clip Duration: **0:47**

## Discussion Questions:

- Why did Professor Robert Crawford accuse Jamal of cheating?
- Did the professor confront Jamal in a healthy, appropriate way? Why or why not?
- Is it easier to assume the best or worst in people? Why?
- What mistakes are made when making assumptions or stereotyping?
- On what do you base your judgements about a person when you first meet them?
- Is there anything wrong with drawing conclusions about a person or situation using just a few bits of information? Explain.
- What can you do to eliminate assumptions, stereotypes and discrimination?

## Movie Title:

# *The Firm*

**Distributed By: Paramount Pictures**
**Year Created: 1993**
**MPAA rating: R**

---

## Plot Summary:

Graduating fifth in his class at Harvard Law, Mitch McDeere has a promising future. After accepting an incredibly enticing package from "The Firm," he begins to uncover the real details about who he is representing and the price others have paid to leave the firm. When the FBI approaches Mitch about working with them, he wonders how he will escape "The Firm" without being disbarred or killed.

## Description of the Scene:

Mitch is in an interview with "The Firm" where they have made a job offer, and it rests in an envelope. Mr. Lambert, a senior partner, challenges Mitch to share the envelope's contents without opening it. Mitch works out the contents of the offer within one minute.

| Topic Area: | Hiring |
| | Human Resource Laws |
| | Problem Solving |
| | Recruiting |

| Start Time: | **2:40** |
| End Time: | **5:50** |
| Clip Duration: | **3:10** |

# Discussion Questions:

- What in this scene is contrary to standard hiring practices today?
- What type of interview was this?
- What type of homework did "The Firm" do to prepare for this interview?
- How did Mitch figure out the contents?
- What made Mitch a good interviewee?
- What do you do to prepare for a candidate interview?
- What interviewing techniques have been most successful for you?
- Have you ever had a bad hire? Good hire? What happened? What will you do differently or the same next time?
- What will you do to prepare when you are interviewing candidates next?

# ■ Movie Title:

## *The Firm*

**Distributed By:** **Paramount Pictures**

**Year Created:** **1993**

**MPAA rating:** **R**

---

## Plot Summary:

Graduating fifth in his class at Harvard Law, Mitch McDeere has
a promising future and several promising offers. After accepting an
incredibly enticing package from "The Firm," he begins to uncover
the real details about who he is representing and the price others have
paid to leave the firm. When the FBI comes to Mitch to make a deal,
he begins to wonder how he will escape "The Firm" without being
disbarred or killed.

## Description of the Scene:

**CAUTION! Start on time. Slight language precedes this clip.**

Mitch has just given the FBI information that will indict each of
the lawyers at "The Firm." FBI agent Wayne Tarrance is at Mitch's
home demanding the rest of the files that will indict members of the
mafia as well. Wayne doesn't understand what seems to be a thin and
meaningless file. Mitch explains that what Wayne has in his hands will
put away each lawyer for mail fraud while giving Mitch an ethical way
out.

■

Topic Area:                    Creativity
                               Problem Solving


Start Time:  **2:25:00**
End Time:  **2:27:00**
Clip Duration:      **2:00**

■ _____

# Discussion Questions:

- What is the truth behind Mitch's argument?
- Is it wrong for Mitch to only give the FBI "The Firm"? Explain.
- What other solutions may Mitch have considered before settling on mail fraud?
- When Wayne asks how Mitch came up with mail fraud and Mitch explains, what does this show about Mitch's ability to problem solve?
- How can creativity solve problems at work or on a team?
- How hard is it to change the way someone thinks?
- When faced with a problem, how do you respond?
- How can you learn to look beyond the first answer or solution you find?

## ■ Movie Title:

# *Forrest Gump*

**Distributed By:** **Paramount Pictures**
**Year Created:** **1994**
**MPAA rating:** **PG-13**

---

## Plot Summary:

This is the story of a simple boy's journey through life. His low IQ of 75 allows him to experience firsthand historical events and political figures, pop culture, business success and more while unaware of their significance. Despite exceeding all expectations for his life, his greatest desire is for his one true love, Jenny, to be with him.

## Description of the Scene:

Forrest is recovering from injuries sustained while fighting in Vietnam. To pass the time, he learns how to play Ping-Pong and his coach simply tells Forrest to "keep your eye on the ball." Forrest quickly becomes a master player because of his amazing ability to focus on the ball.

| Topic Area: | Focus |
| | Goal Setting |
| | Innovative Thinking |
| | Success |

| Start Time: | **58:35** |
| End Time: | **59:45** |
| Clip Duration: | **1:10** |

# Discussion Questions:

- How difficult was it for Forrest to learn how to play Ping-Pong? Why?
- Was Forrest successful? Why or why not?
- How many goals was Forrest trying to achieve at once?
- What is the definition of success?
- How can you relate this clip to goal setting, importance of focus, innovative thinking or keys to success?
- How hard is it to have a large number of goals at one time? Why?
- If you focus on one project or goal, is it easier or harder to accomplish that goal? Explain.
- When multi-tasking, what can you do to maintain your focus with each project or task that needs to be done?

# ■ Movie Title:

## *Freaky Friday*

**Distributed By:** **Walt Disney**
**Year Created:** **2003**
**MPAA rating:** **PG**

---

## Plot Summary:

Dr. Tess Coleman and her teenage daughter, Anna, do not understand each other which leaves them arguing incessantly. One Friday night, they both receive special fortune cookies which cause them to switch bodies the next day. They are literally "walking in the other's shoes" which helps them better understand one another and bridges the generational gap between mom and daughter.

## Description of the Scene:

Anna's mom finds out she was sent to detention and, as a result, takes away all privacy she can think of, including removing her bedroom door. When Anna enters her bedroom, she finds her brother has raided her room, and she is completely ticked off. Finding her mom downstairs, she confronts her, but the conversation doesn't resolve the problem; it only leaves both of them upset.

**Topic Area:**

Communication
Conflict Management
Listening
Respect

| | |
|---|---|
| **Start Time:** | **14:07** |
| **End Time:** | **17:40** |
| **Clip Duration:** | **3:33** |

■

---

# Discussion Questions:

- How did Anna try to resolve conflict? Was she successful? Explain.
- What was Anna really trying to get her mom to understand?
- Why did the conversation leave them both frustrated?
- What could Anna or Tess have done differently?
- Can one talk and listen at the same time? Explain.
- How does it make you feel when you repeatedly get interrupted? Have you ever interrupted others?
- What impact can clear communication and listening have in resolving conflict?
- What steps can you take to be a better listener?
- How can you show respect to those you are in conflict with?

# ■ Movie Title:

## *Gladiator*

**Distributed By: Dreamworks**
**Year Created: 2000**
**MPAA rating: R**

---

## Plot Summary:

Marcus Aurelius is an aging emperor of Rome and realizes the Roman general Maximus is better suited to succeed him, not his own son Commodus. Through the struggle, Maximus and his family are sentenced to death. Maximus escapes death, but the devastating loss of his family is paralyzing; he is captured and sold into slavery as a nameless gladiator.

## Description of the Scene:

As a gladiator, Maximus has just won a great battle in the coliseum and the new emperor Commodus decides to meet this gladiator. The crowd watches as he asks the gladiator, "What is your name?" Maximus' powerful response leaves the coliseum in a deafening roar.

| Topic Area: | Inspiring Others |
| | Leadership |
| | Relationship Building |

| Start Time: | **1:28:30** |
| End Time: | **1:31:40** |
| Clip Duration: | **3:10** |

# Discussion Questions:

- Why did Maximus' response to the emperor leave the coliseum in a roar?
- Why is this scene powerful?
- Why is Maximus inspiring?
- What does this clip show about respect?
- How can you inspire those you work with?
- Is it important to respect a leader? Even one who doesn't appear to deserve it?
- How much power is there in a name?
- Can anyone be a leader? Why or why not?
- What can you do to gain the respect of those you work with?

■ # Movie Title:

## *Gladiator*

**Distributed By: Dreamworks**
**Year Created:  2000**
**MPAA rating:  R**

---

## Plot Summary:

Marcus Aurelius is an aging emperor of Rome and realizes the Roman
general Maximus is better suited to succeed him, not his own son
Commodus. Through the struggle, Maximus and his family are
sentenced to death. Maximus escapes death, but the devastating loss
of his family is paralyzing; he is captured and sold into slavery as a
nameless gladiator.

## Description of the Scene:

**CAUTION! In this scene, there is some violence. Use this clip with
caution and sensitivity to your audience.**

Maximus' true identity is still unknown, and he and the other gladiators
are participating in their first coliseum battle. All the gladiators have a
"self-survival only" mentality. Maximus asks the other gladiators if they
have ever been in the army and shares with the group that they need to
stick together or they will all die. A majority of the men follow his lead
and do as he commands throughout the scene.

■

| Topic Area: | Following |
| | Leadership |
| | Leading Among Peers |
| | Relationship Building |
| | Teamwork |

**Start Time:** **1:24:18**
**End Time:** **1:25:58**
**Clip Duration:** **1:40**

# Discussion Questions:

- Why did the other gladiators follow Maximus?
- What did he command them to do that worked?
- Would the result have been different had they not banded together?
- Why does working together seem counterintuitive to only taking care of yourself? How, in this scene, are they one and the same?
- Have you ever been on a project where the group was not cohesive? What happened?
- What is the value/benefit of working on a team?
- What has helped your team be successful in the past?
- Is there value in following? Explain.
- How can you be a better follower?
- What can you do to strengthen relationships with your peers and clients?

# ■ Movie Title:

# *Glengarry Glen Ross*

**Distributed By: Artisan**
Year Created: **1992**
MPAA rating: **R**

---

## Plot Summary:

The real-estate business is tough for Chicago salesmen, and the new company incentive program is going to push them to close the sale or literally lose their jobs. There is no room for a dry streak if the veteran salesmen want to get the new hot Glengarry leads, which could turn everything around. Just as things start to look up, the office is robbed, including the Glengarry leads, and it is a matter of time before the cops determine who did it.

## Description of the Scene:

**CAUTION! Please review this clip for language. Stop clip on cue – stronger language follows.**

Hot shot executive Blake is brought into the office to motivate a group of veteran sales reps to push them to close deals by teaching them the ABC's (Always Be Closing) of sales. Here Blake tells Shelley "The Machine" Levene to put the coffee down because "coffee is for closers."

■

| Topic Area: | Closing Sales |
| | Goal Setting |
| | Motivation |
| | Sales |

| Start Time: | **7:45** |
| End Time: | **9:06** |
| Clip Duration: | **1:21** |

## Discussion Questions:

- What tactics did Blake use to produce "closers" in the Chicago office? Does this work? Why or why not?
- Blake tells Shelley to put the coffee down, that "coffee is for closers." What does he mean by this?
- How did the sales representatives respond to Blake's tactics? Why?
- What benefits might result if the veteran reps took Blake's advice?
- Is it possible to motivate others? Why or why not?
- Does an incentive program make a difference in motivation?
- How can having specific goals help us achieve more?
- What will it take for you to re-energize yourself in a sales slump?
- What goals do you have for today? This week? Month?

# ■ Movie Title:

## *Glengarry Glen Ross*

**Distributed By: Artisan**
Year Created: **1992**
MPAA rating: **R**

---

## Plot Summary:

The real-estate business is tough for Chicago salesmen, and the new company incentive program is going to push them to close the sale or literally lose their jobs. There is no room for a dry streak if the veteran salesmen want to get the new hot Glengarry leads, which could turn everything around. Just as things start to look up, the office is robbed, including the Glengarry leads, and it is a matter of time before the cops determine who did it.

## Description of the Scene:

Joe and Shelley are picking up the pieces of terrible leads and are back to the grind on the phones. Here they model two completely different styles of selling real estate on the phone.

| Topic Area: | Prospecting |
| | Sales Styles |
| | Sales Questions |

| Start Time: | **18:05** |
| End Time: | **19:30** |
| Clip Duration: | **1:25** |

## Discussion Questions:

- What type of selling/prospecting did the first sales rep (Joe) use? The second (Shelley)?
- Was Joe's selling style persuasive? What worked? What didn't?
- Is one style better than the other? Explain.
- Would either of these examples work today in our company? Explain.
- What are the benefits and drawbacks of selling like this?
- Each of these reps prepared a set of questions to ask their prospects. Is this important? Explain.
- What is the difference between manipulative questioning and consultative sales questioning?
- Just as each of us is unique so are our clients. Should we approach each client in the same manner? Explain.

# ■ Movie Title:

## *Glengarry Glen Ross*

**Distributed By: Artisan**
**Year Created: 1992**
**MPAA rating: R**

## Plot Summary:

The real-estate business is tough for Chicago salesmen, and the new company incentive program is going to push them to close the sale or literally lose their jobs. There is no room for a dry streak if the veteran salesmen want to get the new hot Glengarry leads, which could turn everything around. Just as things start to look up, the office is robbed, including the Glengarry leads, and it is a matter of time before the cops determine who did it.

## Description of the Scene:

Shelley called ahead and made an appointment for both his prospect and her husband to meet with him. He arrives at the prospect's home and only the husband is there. He works his way into the home and starts to pressure-sell the husband.

■

**Topic Area:**　　　Pressure Selling
　　　　　　　　　　Prospecting
　　　　　　　　　　Questioning Sales

| | |
|---|---|
| **Start Time:** | **33:30** |
| **End Time:** | **36:30** |
| **Clip Duration:** | **3:00** |

■

# Discussion Questions:

- What tactics does Shelley use to get his foot in the door, literally, with the prospect?
- Was Shelley professional or unprofessional? Explain.
- Was the prospect comfortable with the situation? Why or why not? What impact could this have?
- Did the prospect trust Shelley? Does it matter?
- Is there anything Shelley could have done differently to get a different result? Discuss.
- Why did Shelley want both husband and wife to be a part of the sales call? Does this tactic work? Explain.
- What is pressure selling? What are the benefits and drawbacks?
- Once in the door of a client (figuratively or literally), what are our next steps?
- What sales techniques have you seen work well in our industry? Why does it work?

■ **Movie Title:**

## *The Guardian*

**Distributed By:** **Touchstone Pictures**
**Year Created:** **2006**
**MPAA rating:** **PG-13**

---

## Plot Summary:

Ben Randall, an aging United States Coast Guard rescue swimmer, is an emotional wreck. After a horrific rescue mission, his commander gives him the choice of quitting or taking a position as an instructor at the USCG training facility in Louisiana. Reluctantly, he takes the position with an 18-week curriculum which fails more than half the students and does not truly prepare candidates for the frontline.

## Description of the Scene:

Randall's class is in a pool filled with ice, and they are freezing. He is walking through points of a rescue mission when the other instructors walk in and criticize his methods. He pointedly tells them why it is important.

**Topic Area:**          Learning Styles
                         Teamwork

**Start Time:**      **46:27**
**End Time:**      **47:27**
**Clip Duration:**      **1:00**

# Discussion Questions:

- Why does Randall make the class get into the freezing cold water?
- Was his method or the old method more effective? Explain.
- How difficult would this type of task be if done alone?
- Why did Randall participate in this task? What does this say to his class?
- If people learn best by experiencing their learning, why are concepts regularly taught by lecture?
- Describe a time when you were encouraged or "pushed" to do better? Was it effective? Why or why not?
- What will you do differently the next time you facilitate a meeting or session to impact different learning styles?

■ # Movie Title:

## *Happy Gilmore*

**Distributed By:** **Universal Studios**
**Year Created:** **1996**
**MPAA rating:** **PG-13**

---

## Plot Summary:

Raised by his grandmother, Happy Gilmore is a wanna-be hockey player with one problem; he can't skate. When his grandmother is told her home will be foreclosed because of unpaid taxes, Happy is persuaded to become a professional golfer. A few people stand in the way of Happy keeping the house, namely Shooter McGavin, the golf tour leader.

## Description of the Scene:

Happy meets with Gary to learn how to harness his negative energy and improve his golf game. Happy is clueless as to what Gary is talking about and what Gary wants him to do.

■

| Start Time: | **35:00** |
| End Time: | **35:45** |
| Clip Duration: | **0:45** |

## Discussion Questions:

- Is there anything wrong with the approach Gary is taking with Happy? If so, what?
- What isn't working in Gary's approach?
- Is Gary a good coach for Happy? Why or why not?
- Have you ever received feedback that didn't seem to make sense? How did it make you feel?
- What should you keep in mind when trying to teach someone?
- What qualities make a good coach?
- What can you do to be a better communicator?
- How can you give and receive feedback effectively?
- Who will you give specific feedback to this week?

## ■ Movie Title:

## *Hoop Dreams*

**Distributed By: Fine Line Features**

**Year Created: 1994**

**MPAA rating: PG-13**

---

## Plot Summary:

Arthur Agee and William Gates are two inner-city Chicago high school students who dream of becoming basketball stars. From freshman year until the start of college, we watch their different lives, struggles, and joys as they each try to achieve their dreams.

## Description of the Scene:

Curtis reflects on his once-amazing career in basketball and how he thought elite athletes could do whatever they wanted and still get play time. When coaches stopped playing him, despite his talent and ability, he quit and became a security guard.

| Topic Area: | Ego |
| | Ownership |
| | Pride |
| | Self-Confidence |
| | Talent |

| | |
|---|---|
| Start Time: | **33:00** |
| End Time: | **34:45** |
| Clip Duration: | **1:45** |

# Discussion Questions:

- What caused Curtis to quit?
- Whose fault was it that Curtis got benched? Explain.
- How long did it take Curtis to realize his mistake?
- Is there such a thing as too much ego? Explain.
- What is the result of having too much ego or pride?
- Share a time when someone made a mistake but didn't take ownership. How did it make you feel?
- When we take responsibility for our actions, what is the result?
- What can you do to keep your pride in check?
- The next time you make a mistake, what can you do to take ownership and make it right?

## ■ Movie Title:

# *Hoosiers*

**Distributed By: Orion Pictures, MGM/UA**
**Year Created: 1986**
**MPAA rating: PG**

---

## Plot Summary:

This film is based on the true story of a small-town Indiana basketball team in 1954 that finds its unlikely way to the state finals. Leading the team is Norman Dale, the volatile head coach, and his assistant, Shooter, the town drunk. Together they inspire their team to greatness, face all the second-guessing townspeople and lead the team to victory.

## Description of the Scene:

**CAUTION! There is foul language right before this clip.**

Norman Dale has been trying to get his assistant coach, Shooter, to get beyond his fears and take the lead. In order for him to really break out of his shell, Norman pulls the referee aside and pretends to be upset. Norman tells the referee to kick him out of the game. This is his way of delegating to Shooter and allowing him to take center stage to build his self-confidence.

■

| Topic Area: | Courage |
| | Delegating |
| | Mentoring |
| | Self-Confidence |

Start Time: **1:04:00**
End Time: **1:07:35**
Clip Duration: **3:35**

# Discussion Questions:

- Why does Coach Dale ask the referee to kick him out?
- Initially, what is Shooter's response?
- What did it take for Shooter to really start coaching?
- As Shooter's mentor, how do you think Coach Dale felt about his risky decision?
- Did this build Shooter's self-confidence? If so, how?
- Why is delegating important?
- Have you ever had someone delegate a task to you and then hover? How did this make you feel?
- When a decision has risk associated with it, how do you make the best decision?
- What can you do to effectively delegate?
- What can you do to push yourself and others to the next level?

## ■ Movie Title:

# *Hoosiers*

**Distributed By: Orion Pictures, MGM/UA**
**Year Created: 1986**
**MPAA rating: PG**

---

## Plot Summary:

This film is based on the true story of a small-town Indiana basketball team in 1954 that finds its unlikely way to the state finals. Leading the team is Norman Dale, the volatile head coach, and his assistant, Shooter, the town drunk. Together they inspire their team to greatness, face all the second-guessing townspeople and lead the team to victory.

## Description of the Scene:

The Hoosiers have made it to the regional finals in Jasper, Indiana and Coach Norman Dale is with his team in the locker room giving them a pep talk. He tells them to not focus on winning or losing, but to focus on the game.

■

| Topic Area: | Coaching |
|---|---|
| | Inspiring Others |
| | Motivation |

| | |
|---|---|
| Start Time: | **1:16:00** |
| End Time: | **1:17:15** |
| Clip Duration: | **1:15** |

---

## Discussion Questions:

- Why does Coach Dale tell the team not to set their sights on the state tournament?
- What does Coach Dale do to focus his team?
- Is Coach Dale believable? Motivational? Inspiring? Explain.
- At work, have you been in a coaching role where you had to give a "pep talk"? What did you do to prepare?
- What qualities make a good coach? Why?
- What motivates or inspires you to do your best at work?
- How are you leaving a legacy?

## ■ Movie Title:

# *How the Grinch Stole Christmas*

**Distributed By: Universal Pictures**
Year Created:  **2000**
MPAA rating:  **PG**

---

## Plot Summary:

The Grinch, a bitter and angry character, is peeved at the thought of Whoville, the nearby village, having a happy time celebrating Christmas. With the Grinch disguised as Santa Claus and his dog diguised as a reindeer, the Grinch raids the village to steal anything that is a part of the holiday. The Grinch believes Whoville is sure to have a sad Christmas this year.

## Description of the Scene:

The Grinch has just stolen all the Whoville gifts and is back at his home looking down on the town Christmas morning; he sees that Christmas still came. His heart grows three sizes.

# Discussion Questions:

- Have you ever experienced a change initiative where one person was like the Grinch? What was that like?
- What typically happens when there is one person not conforming? Can this impact the rest of the group? How?
- Why do some employees resist change?
- Why were the Whos able to embrace change so readily?
- Compare and contrast the Whos and the Grinch.
- Knowing that everyone embraces change at a different pace, how can you help a "Grinch" who is set in his or her ways?

# ■ Movie Title:

## *I Am David*

**Distributed By: Artisan Entertainment**
**Year Created:  2003**
**MPAA rating:  PG**

---

## Plot Summary:

Adapted from Anne Holm's novel, *North to Freedom*, this is the story of 12-year-old boy David who escapes from a concentration camp. With a few instructions to follow and fewer provisions, his only goal is to get a sealed letter to Denmark. This is the journey of a boy who knows nothing of freedom or trust. He now finds himself journeying across Europe alone and learning who he is as a person.

## Description of the Scene:

This is the opening scene of the movie where David is being given specific instructions on how to escape from a concentration camp. If he doesn't follow every instruction exactly, it will cost him his life.

**Start Time:**    **00:40**

**End Time:**    **01:50**

**Clip Duration:**    **1:10**

# Discussion Questions:

- How well do you think David was listening? Why?
- What will happen if he forgets or ignores even one instruction?
- How do you think David is feeling as he listens?
- How often do we listen to others as intently as David was listening? Explain.
- Is there a difference between listening and hearing? Explain.
- What impact can listening have on your job?
- What can you do to become a better listener?

# Movie Title:

## *I Am David*

**Distributed By:** **Artisan Entertainment**
**Year Created:** **2003**
**MPAA rating:** **PG**

---

## Plot Summary:

Adapted from Anne Holm's novel, *North to Freedom*, this is the story of 12-year-old boy David who escapes from a concentration camp. With a few instructions to follow and fewer provisions, his only goal is to get a sealed letter to Denmark. This is the journey of a boy who knows nothing of freedom or trust. He now finds himself journeying across Europe alone and learning who he is as a person.

## Description of the Scene:

Up to this point, David has confided in no one. Here he meets Sophia who has painted his portrait and in exchange for his modeling services has offered lunch to David. As she hangs the portrait she painted, she shares what she sees in it, every bit of which is true. David is surprised at how much a picture speaks and how well she can read him.

Impressions
Nonverbal
Communication

**Start Time:** **1:08:00**
**End Time:** **1:09:30**
**Clip Duration:** **1:30**

# Discussion Questions:

- How and why was Sophia able to tell David so much from just his painting?
- How much was she able to tell David about himself?
- From David's reaction, was her impression accurate? Explain.
- What is nonverbal communication?
- Have you ever given or received the wrong impression from nonverbal communication? What was the result?
- How can you be sure that your expressions are read correctly?
- What can you do to better match your nonverbal communication with what you are really feeling or saying?
- Email doesn't allow the benefit of nonverbal cues. How can you ensure you're communicating your message clearly and receiving the message accurately?

# ■ Movie Title:

## *Karate Kid*

**Distributed By:** **Columbia Pictures**
**Year Created:** **1984**
**MPAA rating:** **PG**

---

## Plot Summary:

Daniel LaRusso has just moved from New Jersey to California and the transition includes bullies and broken promises. Determined to stick up for and prove himself, he learns the art of karate from mentor Mr. Miyagi. While being instructed, he learns that there is much more to karate and life than strength, power and fighting back.

## Description of the Scene:

Daniel learns that karate is something he must do wholeheartedly, that there is no such thing as being lukewarm. Mr. Miyagi tells Daniel that everything he will teach has a purpose and that Daniel must follow without question. After agreeing to whatever Miyagi asks, he is instructed to wax cars by "waxing on" and "waxing off."

**Topic Area:** Coaching
Learning Styles
Mentoring
Training

Start Time: **53:45**
End Time: **56:30**
Clip Duration: **2:45**

■

# Discussion Questions:

- What learning styles are represented in this clip?
- Why did Mr. Miyagi have Daniel wax cars to learn karate?
- Are there other ways Daniel could have learned this lesson? Could it have been more effective? Explain.
- Is Mr. Miyagi a mentor or coach? Explain.
- Have you ever been involved in a simulation to learn a skill? What worked? What didn't work?
- What is the goal of practice?
- What is one discipline or area you want to develop professionally? What will you do to work on that area?
- Identify someone you would like to be mentored or coached by. Identify someone to whom you could offer mentoring or coaching.

## Movie Title:

# *A League of Their Own*

**Distributed By: Columbia Pictures**
**Year Created: 1992**
**MPAA rating: PG**

---

## Plot Summary:

With the majority of American men fighting in World War II, baseball
came to a halt until the AAPGL (All American Pro Girls League)
was created. Kit Keller persuades her sister Dottie Henson to play for
manager Jimmy Dugan. Then Kit's pride gets in the way, and she is
transferred to a competing team.

## Description of the Scene:

A male spectator at one of the AAPGL games makes sexist comments
toward the female ball players. In response to his comments, the
shortstop "mis-throws" and hits him with the ball.

Topic Area:                    Discrimination
                               Sexism

Start Time:    **37:45**
End Time:    **38:15**
Clip Duration:    **0:30**

# Discussion Questions:

- Are the spectator's comments a form of sexism or discrimination? Why or why not?
- Is the shortstop's response to his comments appropriate? Explain.
- What is the difference between sexism and discrimination?
- Is discrimination prevalent in society today? Explain.
- How can differences between sexes, races, ages, etc. be addressed without being sexist, racist, ageist, etc.?
- What can you do when you see or hear something that may be discriminatory or sexist?

# ■ Movie Title:

## *Little Miss Sunshine*

**Distributed By: Fox Searchlight Pictures**
**Year Created: 2006**
**MPAA rating: R**

---

## Plot Summary:

Little Olive Hoover dreams of winning the Little Miss Sunshine contest. Unable to afford other travel, her entire dysfunctional family piles into their Volkswagen mini-bus, along with their neuroses and problems, and begins their road trip to the contest. Along the way, they encounter several set-backs but eventually make it to Redondo Beach where Olive is able to participate in the contest.

## Description of the Scene:

The Hoovers have rushed Richard's father, heroin-snorting Edwin, to the hospital because he didn't wake up that morning. The doctor is about to enter the scene to share the news with the family that Edwin has passed away.

| Topic Area: | Communication |
| | Customer Service |
| | Listening |
| | Problem Solving |
| | Speaking Effectively |

|  |  |
| --- | --- |
| Start Time: | **52:40** |
| End Time: | **55:25** |
| Clip Duration: | **2:45** |

## Discussion Questions:

- Did the doctor use good communication and customer service with the Hoovers? Why or why not?
- Would you have wanted Linda as your bereavement coordinator? Why or why not?
- What did Linda do that was appropriate? Inappropriate?
- Did Linda listen to Richard? Why or why not?
- Did Linda use active listening skills? If so, what were they? If not, what was missing?
- How was Richard attempting to solve a problem? Were his solutions viable?
- Is it important to have empathy and good listening skills in customer service roles? Explain.
- What does "good" customer service look like?
- What can you do to practice good listening?
- What can you do to regularly give the best customer service?

## Movie Title:

# The Lord of the Rings: The Fellowship of the Ring

**Distributed By:** **New Line Cinema**
**Year Created:** **2001**
**MPAA rating:** **PG-13**

## Plot Summary:

In ancient times, the Dark Lord Sauron forged a ring of power to control all of Middle Earth. The ring was taken from him and lost for a very long time until it fell into the hands of Bilbo Baggins, a hobbit from the Shire. The aging Bilbo gives the ring to his young nephew Frodo who takes on the tremendous task of destroying the Ring of Power.

## Description of the Scene:

Frodo and his companions are well into their journey and have already encountered many dangers while trying to get to Mordor to destroy the ring. Frodo slips away from the group and decides to finish the journey on his own. As he pushes off in a boat, Samwise Gamgee races after Frodo and attempts to "swim" after him although he is unable to swim. Frodo watches as Samwise begins to sink.

| Topic Area: | Commitment |
| | Follow Through |
| | Inspiring Others |
| | Motivation |
| | Teamwork |

Start Time: **2:45:25**
End Time: **2:47:38**
Clip Duration: **2:13**

# Discussion Questions:

- Why does Sam attempt to swim out to Frodo although he doesn't know how to swim?
- How do you think this made Frodo feel?
- Sam's assignment from Gandalf earlier in the movie was to complete the journey with Frodo. How can you keep focused on your role and not others' roles?
- During a difficult task or project, is it important to have a "cheerleader"? Why or why not?
- When working with a team, is it easy to follow through with commitments you make? Why?
- What impact does following through with your role and commitments have on a team?
- What can you do to motivate or inspire others?
- What can you do to keep your commitment at work, especially with timelines?

■ Movie Title:

# The Lord of the Rings:
# The Fellowship of the Ring

**Distributed By:** New Line Cinema
**Year Created:** 2001
**MPAA rating:** PG-13

---

## Plot Summary:

In ancient times, the Dark Lord Sauron forged a ring of power to control all of Middle Earth. The ring was taken from him and lost for a very long time until it fell into the hands of Bilbo Baggins, a hobbit from the Shire. The aging Bilbo gives the ring to his young nephew Frodo who takes on the tremendous task of destroying the Ring of Power.

## Description of the Scene:

The rulers of the nations have gathered to determine what should be done with the Ring of Power. The council discusses the history of the ring and how it can be destroyed, bickering about who is the best person for this insurmountable journey and task. In a small meek voice, Frodo volunteers to go, regardless of the sacrifice.

| Topic Area: | Courage |
| | Ego |
| | Leadership |
| | Ownership |

Start Time: **1:29:00**

End Time: **1:31:30**

Clip Duration: **2:30**

# Discussion Questions:

- What is happening between council members in this scene?
- What does this clip show about Frodo and his character?
- What is the significance in Frodo accepting (owning) the charge?
- Does ego ever get in the way of projects? How and why does this happen?
- Are there challenges when working in a team and defining roles? If so, why?
- Would you speak up to accept a challenging role that may require sacrifice? Why or why not?
- Can anyone choose to be a leader? If so, how?
- In what areas of your job could you show more courage?

■ **Movie Title:**

# *The Lord of the Rings: The Return of the King*

**Distributed By:** **New Line Cinema**
**Year Created:** **2003**
**MPAA rating:** **PG-13**

---

## Plot Summary:

Led by Gollum, Frodo and Sam are in the midst of their arduous
journey to Mount Doom to destroy the Ring of Power. Meanwhile,
Aragorn faces his true identity and purpose as the King of Men and
helps to summon the Army of the Dead while Gandalf rides to Minas
Tirith to aid the humans in Sauron's last war against Middle Earth.

## Description of the Scene:

Frodo stands at the edge of Mount Doom having second thoughts
about getting rid of the "precious" ring. Sam urges him to destroy it,
but Frodo doesn't want to get rid of it – he has grown too attached to it
and wants to keep it.

| Topic Area: | Analyzing Issues |
| | Critical Thinking |
| | Problem Solving |

Start Time: **2:39:24**
End Time: **2:41:38**
Clip Duration: **2:14**

# Discussion Questions:

- What is Frodo's problem?
- What caused the problem to exist?
- Why is Frodo having second thoughts about moving forward?
- Is Sam convincing in his plea? What else could he have said to further convince Frodo?
- What should Frodo base his decision on?
- In situations on the job, what causes problems to exist?
- What problem-solving techniques help you make decisions? How?
- What can you change in situations?

# Movie Title:

## *The Majestic*

**Distributed By:** **Warner Brothers**
**Year Created:** **2001**
**MPAA rating:** **PG**

---

## Plot Summary:

Peter Appleton, a script writer in the 1950s, gets blacklisted for being falsely accused as a communist. While driving, he gets into a car accident that leaves him with amnesia. The townspeople that find him mistake him for a war hero and adore him. Eventually, his true identity is revealed.

## Description of the Scene:

Peter and his "staff" are fixing up the Majestic and are in need of some supplies. They go to the city council for help and a townsperson protests that their inquiry is new and out of order. The mayor quickly goes through the process for a motion to follow the rules merely out of legality.

Start Time: **1:19:00**
End Time: **1:20:30**
Clip Duration: **1:30**

# Discussion Questions:

- Why was there an objection to such a simple request?
- Was there any value in going through the motion?
- When it comes to rules, are there times that we should be flexible? Explain.
- Describe a time when you experienced someone at work who was being legalistic. How did it make you and those impacted feel?
- Have you ever been too legalistic? Too permissive?
- Are there times when holding someone accountable for something ridiculously small may be critical? Explain.
- What can you do to work on being less legalistic? Too permissive?

## ■ Movie Title:

## *The Mission*

**Distributed By: Warner Brothers**
**Year Created: 1986**
**MPAA rating: PG**

---

## Plot Summary:

Based on the events surrounding the Treaty of Madrid in 1750, Jesuit missionary Father Gabriel brings Christianity to the mountains of Brazil. Mendoza, a converted slave hunter, joins Father Gabriel in running the mission when Spain sells the colony to Portugal, and together they face Portuguese aggressors while desperately trying to save their mission.

## Description of the Scene:

The cardinal and aristocrats are being serenaded by a young boy. The cardinal praises the boy's talents while an aristocrat responds that it is merely a trick, like that of an animal, and that this boy is not worth as much as a man that is cultured and educated.

■

**Topic Area:**    Discrimination
                   Diversity

| | |
|---:|:---|
| **Start Time:** | **54:15** |
| **End Time:** | **55:45** |
| **Clip Duration:** | **1:30** |

# Discussion Questions:

- In this scene, what is the difference between the boy and the aristocrat and cardinal?
- Why did the aristocrat respond the way he did?
- How does a person's abilities impact the way we think about them?
- What does it mean to stereotype a person? Is this an accurate way to judge other people? Explain.
- What is discrimination? What is diversity?
- When working in diverse environments, what are some things to keep in mind?
- What are the benefits and/or drawbacks to working in a diverse company?

## Movie Title:

# *Monsters, Inc.*

**Distributed By: Walt Disney/Pixar**
**Year Created: 2001**
**MPAA rating: G**

---

## Plot Summary:

James P. Sullivan (Sulley) and Mike Wazowski are two of many monsters that work for Monsters, Inc. generating power from the screams of children. With a little girl accidentally brought into the plant and a devious plan to rid Monstropolis of its power problems, Sulley and Mike have their work cut out for them. Together they will fight for the children they scare every night.

## Description of the Scene:

The scream business is on the decline so Sulley and Mike turn to the laughing business to generate power for the plant.

| Topic Area: | Driving for Results |
|---|---|
| | Flexibility |
| | Innovation |
| | Motivation |

Start Time: **1:20:37**

End Time: **1:22:37**

Clip Duration: **2:00**

---

# Discussion Questions:

- What helped turn around the monsters' problem?
- How many approaches does Mike take to get the child to laugh? Why does Mike keep trying?
- If you were the child, what would you expect from the monster?
- Do you find yourself bringing solutions or problems to the table? Why?
- When you don't get the result you are looking for, what do you do?
- What steps can you take to become more flexible in your job and the way you think?
- What will you do differently the next time you are posed with a problem or challenge?
- What can you do to be more assertive and innovative in your role?

## ■ Movie Title:

# *Mr. Holland's Opus*

**Distributed By: Buena Vista**
**Year Created: 1995**
**MPAA rating: PG**

---

## Plot Summary:

Glenn Holland is a talented musician and composer whose dream is to leave his mark on the world with a truly memorable composition. In the meantime, he takes a job as a teacher to pay the bills. It is in teaching that Glenn learns to deal with his son's handicap and to love him for who he is and not his ability to appreciate music. After 30 years of teaching, his program is cut, and he realizes he has made his mark when his students say farewell by playing *Mr. Holland's Opus.*

## Description of the Scene:

Miss Lang, a former student and the current governor, gives a tribute to Mr. Holland's life and the impact he has made on so many lives. She shares how his life is a living symphony.

**Topic Area:**
Inspiring Others
Recognition

Start Time: **2:08:30**
End Time: **2:11:16**
Clip Duration: **2:46**

# Discussion Questions:

- What impact did Mr. Holland have on his students? Why?
- What does the number of people in the auditorium say about Mr. Holland?
- What makes your team a great team to be part of?
- What or who has inspired you? Why?
- What impact can one person have on a team or work group?
- How do you recognize and inspire others?
- How are you leaving a legacy?

## ■ Movie Title:

# *Mr. Holland's Opus*

**Distributed By: Buena Vista**
**Year Created: 1995**
**MPAA rating: PG**

---

## Plot Summary:

Glenn Holland is a talented musician and composer whose dream is to leave his mark on the world with a truly memorable composition. In the meantime, he takes a job as a teacher to pay the bills. It is in teaching that Glenn learns to deal with his son's handicap and to love him for who he is and not his ability to appreciate music. After 30 years of teaching, his program is cut, and he realizes he has made his mark when his students say farewell by playing *Mr. Holland's Opus.*

## Description of the Scene:

Iris and Glenn are discussing their son Cole and his education. Glenn expresses his concern about the cost when Cole yells for something and begins to throw a fit. When Glenn asks Iris what Cole wants and she doesn't know, she yells, "I want to talk to my son."

Communication
Nonverbal
Communication

Start Time: **1:04:00**
End Time: **1:05:30**
Clip Duration: **1:30**

# Discussion Questions:

- Was Cole trying to communicate?
- What made the conversation with Cole difficult?
- List ways Iris and Glenn could have tried to communicate with their son to understand what he wanted.
- What can this scene teach us about communication?
- What are some challenges with communication at work?
- Is there a "best" practice for communicating at work? Explain.
- List nonverbal ways we communicate at work.
- How does it feel to be misunderstood or not understood at all?
- What problems can arise when we don't communicate clearly?
- What can we do to improve communication skills with others?

## ■ Movie Title:

# *The Muppet Movie*

**Distributed By: Associated Film Distributors**
Year Created:  **1979**
MPAA rating:  **G**

---

## Plot Summary:

Kermit the Frog has been persuaded to make the trek to Hollywood in hopes of making it big. His adventurous journey to Tinseltown includes picking up many other Muppets and evading the restrauteur, Doc Hopper, who wants Kermit to be their new mascot. After multiple run-ins with Doc Hopper, Kermit decides to face his bully and ultimately, with the help of his Muppet friends, he makes it to Hollywood and begins production on his first film.

## Description of the Scene:

Kermit and Miss Piggy are on a date and Steve Martin is their sarcastic waiter.

Start Time: **49:45**

End Time: **51:30**

Clip Duration: **1:45**

# Discussion Questions:

- Did Kermit and Miss Piggy receive good service? Explain.
- Why did the waiter give poor service?
- How does Kermit respond?
- What can this scene tell us about customer service?
- Are there circumstances where this type of customer service is acceptable? Explain.
- How does service influence our thinking?
- How should we react when we feel like dishing out poor service?
- What are things we can do to give the best service possible and drive for results?

# ■ Movie Title:

## *Music of the Heart*

**Distributed By: Miramax**
**Year Created: 1999**
**MPAA rating: PG**

---

## Plot Summary:

A young teacher is determined to teach the beauty of music to underprivileged kids in a Harlem school. The board of education and the "system" come down on her; she loses everything except her determination for the kids' happiness. Her conviction moves her to battle back with inspirational results.

## Description of the Scene:

Roberta, a music teacher, engages in a meeting with a parent and the principal over concerns about her "verbal" abuse. Agreeing to change her ways, she implements a "nicer" Roberta, and her students then tell her to go back to her old ways, because they like the challenge and their old teacher.

| Topic Area: | Feedback |
| --- | --- |
| | Motivation |
| | Performance |
| | Recognition |

| | |
| --- | --- |
| **Start Time:** | **38:58** |
| **End Time:** | **41:40** |
| **Clip Duration:** | **2:42** |

---

## Discussion Questions:

- How did Roberta take the feedback from the principal?
- Was her response appropriate? Why or why not?
- What qualities worked for these students in how Roberta gave feedback?
- What qualities in Roberta's style didn't work for the principal and parent?
- Is recognition important? Why or why not?
- How do you find balance between giving both positive and corrective feedback? Can feedback be corrective and motivating at the same time? If so, how?

■ # Movie Title:

## *Network*

**Distributed By: Warner Brothers**
**Year Created: 1976**
**MPAA rating: R**

## Plot Summary:

Howard Beale is an aging UBS news anchor who is fired due to waning ratings. Beale then announces live that he will commit suicide on air. This sensationalism sends the nightly news program ratings soaring and Howard finds himself with his own series and a slew of followers. The company taking control of UBS finds itself powerless when Howard uses his popularity to make startling revelations about the company.

## Description of the Scene:

Howard Beale shares his opinions about the buyout of UBS. Because it is using Saudi money, Beale says the nation should speak out by sending telegrams to the President. The owner of the station, Arthur Jensen, has called for a private meeting with Howard, hoping to talk some sense into him.

■

| Topic Area: | Conflict Management |
| :--- | :--- |
| | Persuasiveness |
| | Sales |
| | Speaking Effectively |

| | |
| ---: | :--- |
| **Start Time:** | **1:32:15** |
| **End Time:** | **1:35:15** |
| **Clip Duration:** | **3:00** |

## Discussion Questions:

- At the very beginning of the clip, Arthur shared with Howard that previously he was in sales. Why do you think he did this?
- Was Arthur's talk convincing? Why or why not?
- Was there a purpose behind Arthur choosing to have this talk in the conference room? Shades closed? Dramatic presentation? Explain.
- Did Arthur sell Beale on his idea? Why or why not?
- How long should you spend persuading or qualifying a client? Explain.
- Is there an optimal environment for selling your product? If so, what is it?
- Is there an art to persuasion? If so, what qualities would be needed to persuade artfully?
- What can you do to manage conflict successfully?

# ■ Movie Title:

## *Network*

Distributed By: **Warner Brothers**
Year Created: **1976**
MPAA rating: **R**

---

## Plot Summary:

Howard Beale is an aging UBS news anchor who is fired due to waning ratings. Beale then announces live that he will commit suicide on air. This sensationalism sends the nightly news program ratings soaring and Howard finds himself with his own series and a slew of followers. The company taking control of UBS finds itself powerless when Howard uses his popularity to make startling revelations about the company.

## Description of the Scene:

**CAUTION! Please review this clip prior to having groups view for use of profanity.**

Howard Beale has gone slightly out of his mind since hearing he was fired. He decides to go out with a roar and speaks passionately from his heart. He tells the world to shout out, "I'm as mad as hell, and I am not going to take it anymore." People all around the country begin shouting out their windows what they find to be a liberating message.

| Topic Area: | Building Rapport |
| | Inspiring Others |
| | Leadership |
| | Motivation |

| Start Time: | **53:40** |
| End Time: | **57:00** |
| Clip Duration: | **3:20** |

## Discussion Questions:

- Why did the viewers respond to Howard's message?
- What pushed viewers to actually get them out of their chairs, go to their windows and shout out, "I'm as mad as hell, and I am not going to take it anymore."
- How did Howard build rapport with his viewers?
- Would you consider Howard a leader? Why or why not?
- What is the difference between inspiring others and peer pressure?
- What should you do before taking advice from someone?
- Can you motivate others to do something? Why or why not?
- What can you do to inspire and motivate others?
- What do you do to build rapport with others? Give specific examples.

# Movie Title:

## *Network*

**Distributed By: Warner Brothers**
**Year Created: 1976**
**MPAA rating: R**

---

## Plot Summary:

Howard Beale is an aging UBS news anchor who is fired due to waning ratings. Beale then announces live that he will commit suicide on air. This sensationalism sends the nightly news program ratings soaring and Howard finds himself with his own series and a slew of followers. The company taking control of UBS finds itself powerless when Howard uses his popularity to make startling revelations about the company.

## Description of the Scene:

Max Schumacher, UBS nightly news producer, is called into a meeting with Ed, his boss. Max has just allowed Howard to "speak his mind" live on television for his last night of news. Ed is firing Max for his role in allowing this to happen.

Assumptions
Decision Making
Feedback
Ownership
Taking Responsibility

**Start Time:** **20:38**
**End Time:** **22:30**
**Clip Duration:** **1:52**

# Discussion Questions:

- Based on the scene, what assumptions did Max make earlier in the evening? What impact did that assumption have on Max? Did Max take responsibility for his role in that night's broadcast?

- Ed delivered a difficult message to his friend and colleague, Max. What did he do well? Poorly?

- Did Ed's nonverbal communication match his message (firing Max)?

- How difficult would it be to deliver this type of message to someone you have worked with for 20 years? Why?

- When delivering a difficult message, what is important to keep in mind?

- What can you do to avoid making assumptions?

- What can you do to improve your nonverbal skills?

- How can you strive to take responsibility and ownership for your actions?

# ■ Movie Title:

## *Nine Months*

Distributed By: **20ᵗʰ Century Fox**
Year Created: **1995**
MPAA rating: **PG-13**

---

## Plot Summary:

Life for Samuel is turned upside down when his long-time girlfriend Rebecca announces she is pregnant. The thought of fatherhood is unbearable, and the months go by with no change in his attitude. It isn't until Rebecca leaves him that he realizes he is ready to be not only a dad but also a husband.

## Description of the Scene:

Samuel can't believe he is going to have to get rid of his sports car to "make room" for the baby. He reminds Rebecca she said the baby wouldn't change their lives.

**Start Time:** **37:30**
**End Time:** **38:45**
**Clip Duration:** **1:15**

# Discussion Questions:

- What is the validity of this argument?
- What are some solutions to Samuel's problem?
- How can creativity solve problems at work or on a team?
- How hard is it to change the way someone thinks?
- Think of a time when your company went through a change initiative; what worked? What didn't work?
- What can you individually and collectively do to promote change?
- What can you do to learn change skills so that you adapt better?

## ■ Movie Title:

# *North Country*

**Distributed By: Warner Brothers**
**Year Created: 2005**
**MPAA rating: R**

---

## Plot Summary:

Josie Aimes had had enough of her husband's beatings, so she packed up her kids and headed home to the iron range. She begins working at the iron mine. As the daily harassment heightens, she begins speaking out, but management and the union ignore her. After being attacked at work, she quits and files a sexual harassment lawsuit which turns into a class action suit she eventually wins.

## Description of the Scene:

It is Josie's first day at the mine and, during her orientation, her manager makes sexual remarks about the required medical physical she had to have. He makes it clear the mine is not a place for a woman to work.

Harassment
Sexual Harassment

Start Time: **17:00**
End Time: **17:45**
Clip Duration: **0:45**

# Discussion Questions:

- What did Josie's manager do in this scene that could be viewed as sexual harassment? Harassment?
- What can be assumed or implied about his management style for the future?
- What would you have done in her shoes? Explain.
- If this behavior continues, what are Josie's options?
- What is the difference between harassment and sexual harassment?
- Is harassment an issue today?
- If harassment is in the eye of the beholder, what can we do to prevent harassment and sexual harassment?

■ # Movie Title:

## *North Country*

**Distributed By: Warner Brothers**
**Year Created: 2005**
**MPAA rating: R**

---

## Plot Summary:

Josie Aimes had had enough of her husband's beatings, so she packed up her kids and headed home to the iron range. She begins working at the iron mine. As the daily harassment heightens, she begins speaking out, but management and the union ignore her. After being attacked at work, she quits and files a sexual harassment lawsuit which turns into a class action suit she eventually wins.

## Description of the Scene:

Josie goes to her manager to complain about the constant harassment. Her manager tells her to stop complaining, take it like a man and not to bother upper management with the issues.

Start Time:     **29:05**
End Time:     **31:10**
Clip Duration:     **2:05**

# Discussion Questions:

- What did Josie's manager do in this scene that could be viewed as harassment?
- What would you have done in Josie's shoes? Explain.
- What are Josie's options?
- List ways the manager mismanaged the situation.
- As a manager in this situation, what is your role?
- Have you ever known someone in a harassment situation? How did they feel?
- What is harassment?
- What can you do to encourage a harassment-free workplace?

# ■ Movie Title:

## *Ocean's Eleven*

**Distributed By:** **Warner Brothers**
**Year Created:** **2001**
**MPAA rating:** **PG-13**

---

## Plot Summary:

Danny Ocean has just been paroled and already has plotted a $160 million payday at the expense of three casinos. Ocean finds 10 others to work with him and their impossible plan takes life.

## Description of the Scene:

Danny Ocean describes the security system that protects the casino safes they will be robbing. The band of thieves are shocked just thinking about the impossible task ahead.

Analyzing Issues
Problem Solving

Start Time: **30:30**
End Time: **33:30**
Clip Duration: **3:00**

# Discussion Questions:

- What is the reaction of Ocean's crew to the description of the safes?
- Why do they continue to listen to Ocean once they realize it isn't really possible to be successful?
- How did Ocean analyze the task ahead of them?
- Have you ever been given a task at work that stunned you like Ocean's crew? Share.
- Have you ever faced a task or deadline that seemed impossible? Explain.
- Situations that look "impossible" often end up being possible. Why?
- How can you have a solution-minded focus when the task seems impossible?
- What can you do to make a huge job possible?
- What can you do to better analyze a task or situation?

# ■ Movie Title:

## *Ocean's Twelve*

**Distributed By: Warner Brothers**
**Year Created: 2004**
**MPAA rating: PG-13**

---

## Plot Summary:

Three years have passed since "Ocean's Eleven" pulled off a $160 million robbery of three large Reno casinos owned by Terry Benedict. Although insurance paid him back in full, he has found the men that ripped him off and has given them two weeks to come up with the money with interest. While trying to pull off several heists, they encounter a French robber known as "Night Fox" who challenges them to see who is the best thief.

## Description of the Scene:

Linus is one of Ocean's eleven crew members, and he wants to play a bigger role in this heist than the last. He wakes up Rusty to discuss the possibility of doing the negotiation talks with Matsui. He is nervous and stumbles over his request making it evident that he may not be ready. Nonetheless, Rusty gives him the thumbs up, and Linus is overly excited.

■

| Topic Area: | Courage |
| | Negotiation |
| | Nonverbal |
| |    Communication |
| | Speaking Effectively |

| Start Time: | **20:15** |
| End Time: | **22:05** |
| Clip Duration: | **1:50** |

---

# Discussion Questions:

- What did Linus' nonverbals say to Rusty?
- What did Rusty's nonverbals say to Linus?
- What could Linus have done to more effectively communicate his request?
- Linus showed courage. Share a time when you showed courage and the result was surprising.
- What can you learn from this scene?
- Is confidence important when negotiating a request?
- When going before upper management to make a request, what can you do to prepare and build confidence?
- When do you use negotiating in your job? What can you do to better prepare for those negotiations?

## ■ Movie Title:

# *Ocean's Twelve*

**Distributed By: Warner Brothers**
**Year Created: 2004**
**MPAA rating: PG-13**

---

## Plot Summary:

Three years have passed since "Ocean's Eleven" pulled off a $160 million robbery of three large Reno casinos owned by Terry Benedict. Although insurance paid him back in full, he has found the men that ripped him off and has given them two weeks to come up with the money with interest. While trying to pull off several heists, they encounter a French robber known as "Night Fox" who challenges them to see who is the best thief.

## Description of the Scene:

Danny and Rusty have given Linus the chance to take on more of a leadership role as the negotiator in their meeting with Matsui. When Danny, Rusty and Matsui begin to talk in code, Linus looks clueless and begins quoting song lyrics to fit in, making him look ignorant.

Communication
Peer Pressure
Speaking Effectively

| | |
|---|---|
| **Start Time:** | **24:05** |
| **End Time:** | **27:20** |
| **Clip Duration:** | **3:15** |

# Discussion Questions:

- Linus doesn't have a clue what to do and is in over his head. So why does he try to join in using song lyrics?
- What could Linus have done to better present himself?
- Have you ever felt like Linus where you had no clue what people were saying? If so, what happened?
- Why is being unable to communicate frustrating? How do you react in these situations?
- How can you better prepare yourself for situations in which you don't have as much experience?

# ■ Movie Title:

## *Parenthood*

**Distributed By: Universal Pictures**
**Year Created: 1989**
**MPAA rating: PG-13**

---

## Plot Summary:

Gil Buckman is an attorney trying desperately to balance work and home life. His trials include his siblings, rebellious teens, estranged relatives, the "black sheep" of the family and the bizarre.

## Description of the Scene:

Gil's Little League team is about to win their very first game. Kevin, his son, drops the pop fly to lose the game.

| Topic Area: | Laying Blame |
| | Ownership |
| | Taking Responsibility |

| Start Time: | **45:00** |
| End Time: | **46:30** |
| Clip Duration: | **1:30** |

## Discussion Questions:

- Whose fault is the loss of the game? Why?
- What could have been done differently?
- What qualities are both the team and Kevin demonstrating?
- What would taking responsibility look like in this clip?
- Have you ever seen the blame game happen at work? If so, what happened?
- When someone takes ownership of their actions, what is the impact on the person? Group? Others? The company?
- What can you do to take ownership and responsibility for your actions at work?

# ■ Movie Title:

## *Patch Adams*

Distributed By: **Universal Pictures**
Year Created: **1998**
MPAA rating: **PG-13**

---

## Plot Summary:

Hunter Adams admits himself into a mental institution where he discovers his love for helping others. He leaves the institution and vows to become a doctor. His unorthodox methods and pranks get him dismissed, although he is a top student at Virginia Medical College. "Patch" Adams opens the Gesundheit Clinic for the poor but is brought before the Medical Review Board for practicing without a license.

## Description of the Scene:

Patch is in the mental institution talking with his psychiatrist who is more interested in his coffee and sugar than helping Patch with his problems. Patch decides to throw in some off-the-wall information to get a reaction and see how well his psychiatrist is listening.

| Topic Area: | Communication |
| --- | --- |
| | Listening |
| | Nonverbal |
| | Communication |

| Start Time: | **5:58** |
| --- | --- |
| End Time: | **6:53** |
| Clip Duration: | **0:55** |

■ ────────────────────────────────

# Discussion Questions:

- How do you know the psychiatrist was not listening to Patch?
- What does listening have to do with communication?
- Is there a difference between listening and hearing? Explain.
- What kinds of things get in the way of really listening in the workplace or at school?
- How can poor listening lead to problems?
- How do you feel when a co-worker or peer doesn't listen to you?
- What kind of body language do you use when you are really trying to listen and hear what someone is sharing?
- What can we do to be better listeners?
- What can you do to more clearly communicate?

# ■ Movie Title:

## *Patch Adams*

**Distributed By: Universal Pictures**
**Year Created: 1998**
**MPAA rating: PG-13**

---

## Plot Summary:

Hunter Adams admits himself into a mental institution where he discovers his love for helping others. He leaves the institution and vows to become a doctor. His unorthodox methods and pranks get him dismissed, although he is a top student at Virginia Medical College. "Patch" Adams opens the Gesundheit Clinic for the poor but is brought before the Medical Review Board for practicing without a license.

## Description of the Scene:

Patch visits another patient, Arthur, in the mental institution in search of an answer to a brainteaser. The slightly unbalanced professor holds up four fingers and shows that eight fingers appear as you look past yourself to others.

Perspective
Problem Solving

Start Time:  **9:45**
End Time:  **12:06**
Clip Duration:  **2:21**

# Discussion Questions:

- What is the professor's point with the brainteaser?
- How have you found a different perspective at work? What happened?
- When faced with a problem, what do you do? Why?
- How can you learn to look beyond the first answer you see?
- What can you do to come up with an alternate solution to a problem?
- What can you do to voice your alternate ideas and get them heard by the rest of the group?

# Movie Title:

## *Patch Adams*

**Distributed By:** **Universal Pictures**
**Year Created:** **1998**
**MPAA rating:** **PG-13**

## Plot Summary:

Hunter Adams admits himself into a mental institution where he discovers his love for helping others. He leaves the institution and vows to become a doctor. His unorthodox methods and pranks get him dismissed, although he is a top student at Virginia Medical College. "Patch" Adams opens the Gesundheit Clinic for the poor, but is brought before the Medical Review Board for practicing without a license.

## Description of the Scene:

Patch and Truman Schiff pretend to be third-year medical students doing rounds with one of the doctors. The doctor keeps referring to the patient in third person when Patch speaks up and asks for her name. When he says her name, Marjorie beams.

| Topic Area: | Customer Service |
| | Driving for Results |
| | Personalizing |
| | Soft Skills |

| Start Time: | **25:17** |
| End Time: | **26:08** |
| Clip Duration: | **0:51** |

---

# Discussion Questions:

- What is Patch's point in asking the patient's name?
- How did the doctor respond to Patch's question?
  How did Marjorie, the patient, respond?
- How did this simple difference change Marjorie's experience?
- Have you ever been a customer and been treated like Marjorie?
  How did it make you feel?
- How does service influence our thinking?
- How should we react when we feel like dishing out poor service?
- What are things we can do to give the best service possible and
  drive for results?
- What is involved in providing good, better or best customer
  service?
- What small change can you make to make a big difference in
  customer service?

# Movie Title:

## *Pleasantville*

**Distributed By: New Line Cinema**
Year Created: **1998**
MPAA rating: **PG-13**

---

## Plot Summary:

David and Jennifer are twins from the 1990s leading dramatically different lives. One evening, they get sucked back in time (through their television) and find themselves in a 1950s television show as Bud and Mary Sue. Not sure how to return to the 90s, they adapt to their new "Leave it to Beaver" life and bring color to the black and white Pleasantville. After awhile, they begin to wonder if their fast-paced lifestyle is better than the innocence of the past.

## Description of the Scene:

George, a change-averse town father, visits Bud in jail and asks where things went wrong. Bud's response is that nothing went wrong; people change.

**Topic Area:**

Attitude
Change Management
Problem Solving

Start Time: **1:40:00**
End Time: **1:42:00**
Clip Duration: **2:00**

# Discussion Questions:

- What does this scene say about change?
- Is change hard for people? Why or why not?
- When faced with a problem, how do you respond?
- Is change good? Why or why not?
- With business initiatives constantly undergoing change, how can you make the process better or easier?
- Think about a change you're currently experiencing. What parts of the old process are you or someone you know clinging to? Is this helpful?

# ■ Movie Title:

## *Pride and Prejudice*

**Distributed By:** **Focus Features**
**Year Created:** **2005**
**MPAA rating:** **PG**

---

## Plot Summary:

The five Bennet sisters have been raised to believe their sole purpose in life is finding a husband. Strong-willed Lizzie is determined to marry only for love. When wealthy bachelor Mr. Bingley takes up residence nearby, the Bennets are delighted and hoping several of his sophisticated friends are eligible suitors! When Lizzie meets the wealthy but proud Darcy, she swears to loathe him forever.

## Description of the Scene:

Lizzie is visiting her dear friend, and they are at Lady Catherine de Bourgh's home for dinner. While eating, Lady Catherine asks inappropriate questions, and Lizzie puts her subtly in her place by not responding directly to the questions.

Start Time: **1:00:33**
End Time: **1:02:11**
Clip Duration: **1:38**

# Discussion Questions:

- Were Lady Catherine's questions appropriate? Explain.
- Was Lizzie's response appropriate or respectful? Why or why not?
- What impact did the environment, and those at the dinner table, have on the conversation?
- What consequences did Lizzie have to contemplate before her response, if any?
- Does Lady Catherine's position give her the authority to speak her mind openly? Explain.
- What impact do others have on our behavior?
- Do circumstances influence what we do or how we solve a problem or address a conflict?
- When put on the spot to answer a pointed question at work, what should we do? What steps might we take to analyze the situation before responding?

# ■ Movie Title:

# *Pride and Prejudice*

**Distributed By: Focus Features**
**Year Created: 2005**
**MPAA rating: PG**

## Plot Summary:

The five Bennet sisters have been raised to believe their sole purpose in life is finding a husband. Strong-willed Lizzie is determined to marry only for love. When wealthy bachelor Mr. Bingley takes up residence nearby, the Bennets are delighted and hoping several of his sophisticated friends are eligible suitors! When Lizzie meets the wealthy but proud Darcy, she swears to loathe him forever.

## Description of the Scene:

Elizabeth Bennet and Mr. Darcy are having a heated discussion in the rain. Mr. Darcy shares candidly that he cares for her, but also shares some behavior of Lizzie's he has found disappointing. Lizzie blasts Darcy with accusations. Darcy takes ownership for his actions and gives an explanation. Deep down Lizzie likes Darcy but is hurt by the false assumptions she has made about him.

Assumptions
Feedback
Ownership

Start Time: **1:08:30**
End Time: **1:12:15**
Clip Duration: **3:45**

# Discussion Questions:

- What assumptions were made by Lizzie? By Darcy?
- Did Darcy take ownership for his actions?
  What worked or didn't work?
- Were Darcy's statements fair? Explain.
- Did Darcy give Lizzie feedback appropriately? Why or why not.
- Did Lizzie give Darcy feedback appropriately? Explain.
- What problems can be caused when assumptions are made?
- Should we give feedback the same way to everyone? Explain.
- What problems could arise from giving feedback the same way to others?
- Is feedback important? Why or why not?
- What strategies can we use for giving and receiving feedback?

# ■ Movie Title:

## *The Pursuit of Happyness*

**Distributed By:** **Columbia Pictures**
**Year Created:** **2006**
**MPAA rating:** **PG-13**

---

## Plot Summary:

It is 1981, and Chris Gardner is a struggling salesman desperate to make ends meet. In his attempt for a better life, he applies for an unpaid stockbroker internship with the hope of being selected at the end of class for a fulltime career. His wife's built-up bitterness explodes when she hears his latest plan, and she leaves him and their son. Father and son struggle through homelessness, tax seizure and despair as they journey to see their dreams come to fruition.

## Description of the Scene:

Chris has just spent the night in jail for unpaid parking tickets. He gets released just in time to run to his interview in the hope of getting a stockbroker internship. He is led into the interviewing room, dressed in his painting attire, where he is candid and upfront during the interview process.

■

| Topic Area: | Hiring |
| --- | --- |
| | Impressions |
| | Interviewing |
| | Perseverance |
| | Speaking Effectively |

| Start Time: | **43:00** |
| --- | --- |
| End Time: | **45:45** |
| Clip Duration: | **2:45** |

# Discussion Questions:

- How did Chris speak effectively in this interview?
- What questions and opinions did he share to participate proactively?
- When the interviewing team first saw Chris, what was their reaction?
- What type of interview was this? Were the interviewers objective during the process?
- Would you have given Chris a chance with this first impression? Why?
- Have you ever been in a situation where you had to think and speak on your feet? What happened?
- Have you ever wanted to walk away and not face a situation because of circumstances? What can you do to work on persevering and overcoming negative self-talk?
- How can you be more objective in the interview process?

## ■ Movie Title:

# *The Pursuit of Happyness*

**Distributed By:** **Columbia Pictures**
**Year Created:** **2006**
**MPAA rating:** **PG-13**

---

## Plot Summary:

Chris Gardner is a struggling salesman desperate to make ends meet. In his attempt for a better life, he applies for an unpaid stockbroker internship with the hope of being selected at the end of class for a fulltime career. His wife's built-up bitterness explodes when she hears his latest plan and she leaves him and their son. Father and son struggle through homelessness, tax seizure and despair as they journey to see their dreams come to fruition.

## Description of the Scene:

Chris and his son, Christopher, are shooting hoops when his son says he wants to be a basketball star. Chris tells him that if he inherited his skills then Christopher should stop thinking about that. Christopher feels his dreams have been shot down, and he throws the ball. Chris realizes what he said was wrong and tells Christopher not to let others decide your dreams and future.

Goal Setting
Inspiring Others
Motivation
Relationship Building

| | |
|---|---|
| **Start Time:** | **54:00** |
| **End Time:** | **55:45** |
| **Clip Duration:** | **1:45** |

# Discussion Questions:

- What is Christopher's dream?
- Why did Chris shoot it down?
- After thinking about what he told his son, he changed his mind. Why?
- How could this conversation positively and negatively affect father and son?
- What is the difference between a dream and a goal?
- Can you inspire and motivate others? Why or why not?
- Have you ever had someone shoot down an idea you had? How did it make you feel?
- Part of inspiring others is recognizing individual and team success. Think of someone you can recognize this week and share what you will do.

## ■ Movie Title:

# *Remember the Titans*

**Distributed By: Walt Disney Productions**
**Year Created: 2000**
**MPAA rating: PG**

---

## Plot Summary:

T.C. Williams High School is being forced to integrate under federal mandate. The white head coach is displaced by Herman Boone who is black. Tension arises as two races come together on the field. During their two-week training, many barriers fall away and the team begins to unite and, as the perfect season progresses, the community learns to accept these changes as well.

## Description of the Scene:

Gerry (a white player) and Julius (a black player) are supposed to learn something about each other and get into a heated discussion. Gerry berates Julius, because he did not cover for the team. Julius responds by saying that, as the Captain, Gerry should be a leader and a leader would get his original teammates to cover for his new teammates.

■

| Topic Area: | Attitude |
| | Leadership |
| | Teamwork |

| Start Time: | **29:15** |
| End Time: | **30:47** |
| Clip Duration: | **1:32** |

■ ───────────────────────────────

# Discussion Questions:

- Julius asks Gerry if, as a Captain, he was also a leader and Gerry says yes. Do you agree with this? Why or why not?
- Julius has a bad attitude about the team; is this a reflection of poor leadership?
- Why is it important to respect a leader?
- Have you ever been on a project where the group was not cohesive? What happened?
- What is the value/benefit of working on a team?
- What has helped your team be successful in the past?
- What can you do to be a leader?
- How can you manage your attitude during challenging times?

## ■ Movie Title:

## *Remember the Titans*

**Distributed By:** **Walt Disney**
**Year Created:** **2000**
**MPAA rating:** **PG**

## Plot Summary:

T.C. Williams High School is being forced to integrate under federal mandate. The white head coach is displaced by Herman Boone who is black. Tension arises as two races come together on the field. During their two-week training, many barriers fall away and the team begins to unite and, as the perfect season progresses, the community learns to accept these changes as well.

## Description of the Scene:

Before dawn, Coach Boone gets all of the guys up for a run. The team finishes at the battlefield of Gettysburg. He then gives a motivational talk about how it was on this field that 50,000 men died fighting the same battle they are fighting on the field—racism.

■

| Topic Area: | Coaching |
| | Inspiring Others |
| | Motivation |
| | Racism |
| | Teamwork |

| Start Time: | **31:00** |
| End Time: | **34:00** |
| Clip Duration: | **3:00** |

# Discussion Questions:

- What purpose did Coach Boone have for taking the team out for a run at 3 a.m.? What impact did it have on the discussion?
- How does Coach Boone use the past to teach? Is it effective? Explain.
- Why was Coach Boone inspiring?
- What causes racist attitudes? Why is this destructive?
- Have you ever been on a project where the group was not cohesive? What happened?
- What impact can one person have in motivating a team or group?
- Share a story about someone who has inspired you. What lasting impact did it have?
- What is the value/benefit of working on a team?
- What has helped your team be successful in the past?
- What can you do to motivate or inspire others?

## ■ Movie Title:

# *Robots*

**Distributed By:** **20<sup>th</sup> Century Fox**
**Year Created:** **2005**
**MPAA rating:** **PG**

---

## Plot Summary:

In a world of robots, Rodney proves to be anything but average when it comes to inventions. Rodney moves to Robot City to make his dreams of inventing come true at Bigweld Industries. When he gets there, he finds Bigweld has been forced out of his position by Ratchet who is motivated by profit. Rodney and his new friends try to find a way to get Bigweld back in his position to save the robot population from being recycled.

## Description of the Scene:

The Copperbottoms are watching the Bigweld show. Rodney is amazed and feels like Bigweld is talking to him. Bigweld talks about how inventions come about: brainstorming ideas, seeing a need and then filling that need.

| Topic Area: | Brainstorming |
| | Ideas |
| | Motivation |
| | Inspiring Others |

| Start Time: | **5:40** |
| End Time: | **7:15** |
| Clip Duration: | **1:35** |

# Discussion Questions:

- Is Bigweld inspiring? Why or why not?
- Why is Rodney fascinated with Bigweld?
- How did Rodney feel while he was watching the show?
- What impact did a stranger have on Rodney?
- What is your initial reaction to this clip?
- Are there others around you that look up to you?
- Bigweld says, "See a need, fill a need;" how can we apply that?
- What motivates or inspires you to do your best work?
- What can we do to support others in trying something new or looking to fill the need?
- How can we be more solution-focused versus problem-focused?

# ■ Movie Title:

# *Rocky*

**Distributed By:** **United Artists**
**Year Created:** **1976**
**MPAA rating:** **PG**

## Plot Summary:

A Philadelphia meat factory worker, Rocky Balboa, dreams of a better life as a boxer. When heavyweight champion Apollo Creed visits Philadelphia, his managers set up an exhibition for an amateur to debut and have a shot at becoming known in the boxing world. Rocky has this one shot at making it big and trains passionately for the opportunity.

## Description of the Scene:

Rocky is training for his match. His deep desire to be the best is shown as he uses a wide variety of physical training to help him prepare.

| Topic Area: | Discipline |
| | Perseverance |
| | Self-Control |
| | Training |

Start Time: **1:30:30**
End Time: **1:33:00**
Clip Duration: **2:30**

# Discussion Questions:

- What qualities does Rocky show in this scene?
- How important is it for Rocky to train?
- How does Rocky show self-discipline?
- What value is there in training for personal growth?
- How do you train for the challenges in your job?
- In what areas of your job do you lack self-control and discipline?
- When tired of improving and working toward the same goal, what can you do to persevere?
- How can you improve your self-control and discipline?

# ■ Movie Title:

## *Runaway Bride*

**Distributed By:** **Paramount Pictures**
**Year Created:** **1999**
**MPAA rating:** **PG**

---

## Plot Summary:

Ike Graham has problems with writer's block, an ex-wife and getting his text in on time. Maggie also has a problem—cold feet and literally leaving men at the altar. Ike loses his job after writing an offensive, exaggerated story on Maggie. The only way to get his job back is with a fact-based story on Maggie. While in town to cover her fourth wedding, he falls for her.

## Description of the Scene:

Members of Maggie's wedding party are giving her a hard time for continually getting cold feet at the altar. Ike is giving a toast to the wedding party and stands up for her.

| Topic Area: | Conflict Management |
| --- | --- |
| | Feedback |
| | Judging |
| | Making Mistakes |

Start Time: **1:10:45**
End Time: **1:13:00**
Clip Duration: **2:15**

# Discussion Questions:

- What is the conflict in this scene?
- Is the wedding party giving feedback in an appropriate manner? Explain.
- Why do people judge others?
- As a peer, is it alright to judge another's work? Explain.
- Have you made a mistake others remind you about? How does it make you feel?
- What is the best thing to do when you have made a mistake?
- Can feedback be corrective and motivating at the same time? If so, how?
- How do you find balance between giving both positive and corrective feedback?

## ■ Movie Title:

# *Shrek*

**Distributed By: Dreamworks**
**Year Created: 2001**
**MPAA rating: PG**

---

## Plot Summary:

Shrek is an ogre who is feared by all people. He lives in a swamp, minding his own business, until one day his swamp is turned into a refugee camp for fairy-tale beings. To save his swamp, Shrek and Donkey must save Princess Fiona and bring her back to become Farquaad's wife. Along the way, Shrek falls in love with Fiona.

## Description of the Scene:

Donkey and Shrek are arguing outside Shrek's home in the swamp. Donkey wants to hold Shrek accountable for his behavior; Shrek pushes others away and doesn't want to accept anyone's love or friendship.

Start Time: **1:11:44**
End Time: **1:12:37**
Clip Duration:     **0:53**

# Discussion Questions:

- What is Donkey's risk in telling Shrek what he thinks?
- Is Donkey telling the truth?
- Is Shrek listening to Donkey?
- What conflict is brewing between Donkey and Shrek?
- Can two people see the same event and feel differently about it? Explain.
- How do past experiences influence how we feel about an event?
- Why is it important to see things from another's point of view?
- How can listening and understanding help to resolve a conflict?
- When you realize that you are amidst a conflict, how can you adjust your critical path?

## ■ Movie Title:

## *Shrek*

**Distributed By: Dreamworks**
**Year Created: 2001**
**MPAA rating: PG**

## Plot Summary:

Shrek is an ogre who is feared by all people. He lives in a swamp, minding his own business, until one day his swamp is turned into a refugee camp for fairy-tale beings. To save his swamp, Shrek and Donkey must save Princess Fiona and bring her back to become Farquaad's wife. Along the way, Shrek falls in love with Fiona.

## Description of the Scene:

Donkey and Shrek have just saved Fiona from the dragon, and Fiona asks to see her rescuer's face as it is destiny that he be her true love. Donkey and Shrek laugh hysterically at the thought of Shrek being her true love. When Shrek takes off his helmet to reveal he is an ogre, she's upset because she assumed he was a prince.

**Topic Area:**  Assumptions
Expectations

Start Time:  **40:15**
End Time:  **43:15**
Clip Duration:  **3:00**

# Discussion Questions:

- What assumptions did Fiona make?
- What did Fiona base her assumptions on?
- When Shrek took off his helmet, what was Fiona's reaction? Why did she react the way she did?
- What happens when we have expectations that are not met?
- What types of assumptions are made at work? What impact can that have—both positive and negative—on a business?
- What can you do to avoid making assumptions?

# ■ Movie Title:

## *Sister Act*

**Distributed By: Touchstone Pictures**
**Year Created: 1992**
**MPAA rating: PG**

---

## Plot Summary:

Delores Van Cartier is a lounge singer in Reno, Nevada looking to make it big. Instead, she witnesses a murder that was ordered by her mob boss boyfriend, Vince. In order to keep her alive to testify, the police send her into hiding at a convent as Sister Mary Clarence. While there, she turns the tired, lifeless choir into a hip-hop contemporary choir that attracts more attention.

## Description of the Scene:

The nuns are in need of a helicopter in order to save Sister Mary Clarence from a tragedy, but they can't afford one. While praying out loud for God's mercy on the pilot's soul, the nuns follow the pilot even though he has refused to help them. He is quickly persuaded to aid their cause.

Helping Others
Persuasiveness
Problem Solving
Speaking Effectively

Start Time: **1:21:30**
End Time: **1:22:30**
Clip Duration: **1:00**

# Discussion Questions:

- What was the nuns' problem?
- How did they persuade the pilot to change his mind?
- Have you ever been persuaded to change your mind? Explain.
- Is there an art to persuasion? Explain.
- Have you ever been asked to help on a project that wasn't yours, and you didn't really want to? How did it make you feel?
- Has someone helped you when it wasn't his or her project? How did it make you feel? What were the results?
- Describe a time when someone communicated clearly. What made it so easy to understand?
- What can you do to practice speaking more effectively?
- How can you become more persuasive?

# ■ Movie Title:

## *Sister Act*

**Distributed By: Touchstone Pictures**
**Year Created: 1992**
**MPAA rating: PG**

---

## Plot Summary:

Delores Van Cartier is a lounge singer in Reno, Nevada looking to make it big. Instead, she witnesses a murder that was ordered by her mob boss boyfriend, Vince. In order to keep her alive to testify, the police send her into hiding at a convent as Sister Mary Clarence. While there, she turns the tired, lifeless choir into a hip-hop contemporary choir that attracts more attention.

## Description of the Scene:

The convent choir is "singing" during a church service. The few churchgoers in the audience have little energy and enthusiasm for the hymns, and the final solo is completely uninspiring.

**Topic Area:**

Expectations
Inspiring Others
Motivation
Performance

| | |
|---|---|
| **Start Time:** | **30:30** |
| **End Time:** | **32:30** |
| **Clip Duration:** | **2:00** |

---

# Discussion Questions:

- What made this uninspiring?
- In this scene, do you think boredom is contagious? Explain.
- Are the nuns working well as a team? Why or why not?
- What is the choir's job or purpose? Did they meet expectations? Explain.
- Have you been on a project where the group was not cohesive? What happened?
- Share a story about someone who has inspired you. What lasting impact did it have?
- What is the value/benefit of working on a team?
- What impact can one person have in motivating a team or group?
- What has helped your team be successful in the past?
- What can you do to meet and exceed expectations?
- What can you do to motivate or inspire others?

# ■ Movie Title:

## *Six Days, Seven Nights*

**Distributed By: Buena Vista Pictures**
**Year Created: 1998**
**MPAA rating: PG-13**

---

## Plot Summary:

An ambitious New York journalist, Robin, and her boyfriend head to
the South Pacific on a romantic getaway. While there, Robin gets a call
from her boss to cover a story on a nearby island. Robin can't resist her
boss and, unfortunately, the only plane available to make the trip is
piloted by the formidable Quinn Harris. En route, the plane crashes on
an uninhabited island with little chance of rescue.

## Description of the Scene:

Robin and her boyfriend survey the puddle jumper they must take to
get to their vacation destination. Not sure of its ability to even take off,
they must trust the pilot as there are no alternatives.

| | |
|---|---|
| **Start Time:** | **5:45** |
| **End Time:** | **7:15** |
| **Clip Duration:** | **1:30** |

---

# Discussion Questions:

- Would you have gotten on Quinn's plane? Why or why not?
- What was the basis for Robin and Frank's decision to charter the plane?
- How important is the analysis phase of a project, task or program? Why?
- How much time do you spend analyzing decisions? Is it enough? Why or why not?
- What can you do to modify circumstances when forced to decide between two bad options?
- How do you weigh your decisions at work?
- What will you do in your next project to better prepare, analyze scope and make decisions?

# ■ Movie Title:

## *Stand and Deliver*

**Distributed By:** **Warner Brothers**
**Year Created:** **1988**
**MPAA rating:** **PG**

---

## Plot Summary:

Jaime Escalante is a math teacher in an inner-city school in East Los Angeles, California. With unconventional teaching methods, he takes 18 students and gives them a chance to prove their abilities. Despite naysayers, they take an Advanced Placement calculus exam. With all 18 scoring off the charts, testing officials disqualify their scores and call them cheaters. The only way to prove themselves is to take an even more difficult exam.

## Description of the Scene:

Mr. Escalante breaks the news to his students that they will only have one day to review for the retake exam. As he tries to offer encouragement, he pauses and moves into an inspiring and motivational moment with his students.

■

| Topic Area: | Inspiring Others |
| --- | --- |
| | Leadership |
| | Mentoring |
| | Motivation |

| Start Time: | 1:26:45 |
| --- | --- |
| End Time: | 1:27:45 |
| Clip Duration: | 1:00 |

# Discussion Questions:

- Why does Mr. Escalante's speech work with the students?
- Is Mr. Escalante being a mentor or a coach? How?
- How did Mr. Escalante get the students to agree?
- What is appealing about Mr. Escalante's style?
- What was the roadblock the students had and how did they handle it?
- Think of a time you were in this role. What worked? What didn't? What will you do differently next time?
- Have you ever been on a team that didn't handle challenges well? What was that like? Is there anything that could have been done differently? If so, what?

## ■ Movie Title:

## *Stand and Deliver*

Distributed By: **Warner Brothers**
Year Created:  **1988**
MPAA rating:  **PG**

## Plot Summary:

Jaime Escalante is a math teacher in an inner-city school in East Los
Angeles, California. With unconventional teaching methods, he takes
18 students and gives them a chance to prove their abilities. Despite
naysayers, they take an Advanced Placement calculus exam. With all
18 scoring off the charts, testing officials disqualify their scores and
call them cheaters. The only way to prove themselves is to take an even
more difficult exam.

## Description of the Scene:

The scene opens with Mr. Escalante walking home, assuming that his
car has been stolen. Jaime has second thoughts about teaching these
unlikely students calculus and his decision to quit his job as an engineer.
His wife sticks up for his students when he hears his students and sees
they have fixed up his car, not stolen it.

■

Assumptions
Discrimination
Diversity

Start Time: **1:17:54**
End Time: **1:21:24**
Clip Duration: **3:30**

# Discussion Questions:

- What assumptions were made in this scene?
- What was the impact of those assumptions?
- What role did the students' backgrounds and culture play in making assumptions?
- Were there any underlying prejudices? If so, what were they?
- What types of prejudices do you see in the workplace? Is there prejudice against over/underweight people?
- What was the significance when the students brought the car back fixed up?
- Have you ever seen someone (perhaps even yourself) prejudge a person and their abilities on a project? What impact did that have?

## ■ Movie Title:

# *Superman*

**Distributed By: Warner Brothers**
**Year Created: 1978**
**MPAA rating: PG**

## Plot Summary:

With the planet of Krypton doomed, Jor-El sends his infant son, Superman, to Earth for refuge. Superman grows up as Clark Kent and learns that he possesses superpowers which he hides from those around him but uses to keep peace and derail the evil Lex Luthor's plan to detonate nuclear bombs.

## Description of the Scene:

Clark tells his ma that it is time for him to leave even though he doesn't know where he is headed. Although he doesn't want to leave, he knows he must.

**Start Time:** **39:00**
**End Time:** **40:45**
**Clip Duration:** **1:45**

# Discussion Questions:

- Why would Clark leave his comfort zone for something completely unknown to even himself?
- Why is change difficult?
- What is the most difficult change you have had to face at work? What did you do to embrace the change?
- In business, change is inevitable for success, and at times it may seem as though companies change too fast. What can you do to drive change?
- Review changes in your career. What were sources of discomfort? How can this information help you with future changes?

# Movie Title:

# *A Time To Kill*

**Distributed By: Wynwood Press**
**Year Created: 1989**
**MPAA rating: R**

## Plot Summary:

Carl Lee Hailey's 10-year-old daughter was raped and beaten by two white men. As they walk into the courthouse, Carl Lee guns the men down. Lawyer Jake Brigance has accepted the toughest case of his career—defending this black man in Mississippi accused of murder. Throughout the case, racial hatred heightens, with an all-white jury, the Klu Klux Klan and the NAACP. Jake risks everything by attempting to win the case.

## Description of the Scene:

Jake meets with Judge Omar Noose to discuss a change of venue for the accused in order to have a better chance of a fair trial. Judge Noose denies the change and tells Jake that he won't be getting an appeal. He tells Jake that defending a black murderer is unpopular and to think about backing out.

| Topic Area: | Negotiation |
|---|---|
| | Risk Taking |

Start Time: **1:07:25**

End Time: **1:09:15**

Clip Duration: **1:50**

■

---

# Discussion Questions:

- Why is the judge denying Jake's request for a change of venue?
- When Jake tries to negotiate with the judge, what happens?
- When Judge Omar tells Jake not to bother with an appeal, what does this show about Omar?
- Omar encourages Jake to back away from the case stating that it is unpopular. Why?
- Why is it important to take risks?
- Have you ever tackled a problem that was unpopular? What was the result?
- What issues or problems have come up that others do not want to tackle? Why has no one taken it on? How can you keep the risk manageable?
- When faced with a task that involves risk, what do you do?

■

## ■ Movie Title:

# *A Time To Kill*

**Distributed By: Wynwood Press**
**Year Created: 1989**
**MPAA rating: R**

## Plot Summary:

Carl Lee Hailey's 10-year-old daughter was raped and beaten by two white men. As they walk into the courthouse, Carl Lee guns the men down. Lawyer Jake Brigance has accepted the toughest case of his career—defending this black man in Mississippi accused of murder. Throughout the case, racial hatred heightens, with an all-white jury, the Klu Klux Klan and the NAACP. Jake risks everything by attempting to win the case.

## Description of the Scene:

It is the night before final summations, and Jake is meeting with Carl to tell him his chances of going free is minute at best but reassures Carl of their friendship. Carl quickly responds with, "We ain't friends, Jake! I ain't never seen you in my part a town!" Jake realizes that although he feels like he has a connection with the black community in his Southern town, he really doesn't. Carl talks about the differences between black and white.

■

| Topic Area: | Assumptions |
| | Biases |
| | Diversity |
| | Prejudice |
| | Stereotype |

| | Side 2 |
| Start Time: | 52:55 |
| End Time: | 55:45 |
| Clip Duration: | 2:55 |

# Discussion Questions:

- What assumptions is Jake making about the case?
- Is Jake listening to Carl? If so, share what he is doing to model listening.
- Carl suggests that Jake is prejudiced and can't see beyond the color of his skin; what does he mean by this?
- Is there truth to what Carl is saying? Explain.
- Is it important for you to know your own cultural values and background? Others? Why or why not?
- Describe a time when making an assumption had a negative impact. A positive impact.
- What types of bias and prejudice could arise at work?
- What can you do to be proactive and think beyond color, size, ability, etc.?

# ■ Movie Title:

## *Tin Men*

**Distributed By: Touchstone**
**Year Created: 1987**
**MPAA rating: R**

---

## Plot Summary:

Being an aluminum siding salesman in the 60s, a tin man, is where the money is at. When Bill "BB" Babowsky drives his new car off the lot and hits another tin man from a competing company, Ernest Tilley, the rivalry begins. Amidst the rivalry, the home improvement commission is uprooting corrupt sales practices; both men have their licenses revoked.

## Description of the Scene:

Bill Babowsky heads out on a sales call where he and his partner decide to run a "Life Magazine" pitch on a potential client. Ultimately, three salesmen run the creative "scam" together to close the deal.

**Start Time:**    **12:50**
**End Time:**    **16:25**
**Clip Duration:**    **3:35**

# Discussion Questions:

- What is the sales pitch BB is using?
- Although they weren't truthful in their approach, what are the elements in this pitch that make it work?
- Why do the salesmen work as a team? Is this valuable? Explain.
- What lessons can you take away from this scene?
- How did these two men "qualify" their prospect in this scene?
- What is the most powerful thing you do in sales?
- What are the most important aspects to qualifying or disqualifying a prospect in our business?

## ■ Movie Title:

# *Tin Men*

**Distributed By: Touchstone**
**Year Created: 1987**
**MPAA rating: R**

---

## Plot Summary:

Being an aluminum siding salesman in the 60s, a tin man, is where the money is at. When Bill "BB" Babowsky drives his new car off the lot and hits another tin man from a competing company, Ernest Tilley, the rivalry begins. Amidst the rivalry, the home improvement commission is uprooting corrupt sales practices; both men have their licenses revoked.

## Description of the Scene:

At the offices of the Gibraltar Aluminum Company, the salesmen discuss creative ways to learn about their prospect. The men share their tactics for reading their clients and understanding what they are up against.

■

**Topic Area:** Sales

| | |
|---|---|
| **Start Time:** | **24:25** |
| **End Time:** | **26:38** |
| **Clip Duration:** | **2:13** |

# Discussion Questions:

- What tactics do the salesmen share for getting to know prospects?
- Considering it was the 1960s, is there any truth to their tactics for that time period?
- Is there anything wrong with the way they determine the effort they will put into the call?
- What do we do today to better understand our prospect?
- When we have a client that has a longer buying cycle, how do we determine when to cut our losses or disqualify?
- What happens when we underestimate a prospect?
- What can you do to eliminate assumptions about prospects?

## ■ Movie Title:

## *Twister*

**Distributed By: Warner Brothers**
**Year Created:  1996**
**MPAA rating:  PG-13**

---

## Plot Summary:

Bill is trying to get his wife Jo to sign divorce papers so he can marry his new girlfriend when a series of amazing storms sweep across Oklahoma. They put their broken marriage on the backburner and begin to battle fierce tornados in an attempt to create a better warning system.

## Description of the Scene:

Jo confronts Jonas on being too close to the tornado, but he blatantly disregards her and suffers fatal consequences for not heeding her advice.

Topic Area:                    Confrontation
                               Listening
                               Risk Taking

Start Time:  **1:31:45**
End Time:    **1:34:15**
Clip Duration:    **2:30**

---

# Discussion Questions:

- Why didn't Jonas listen?
- Did Jonas calculate the risk involved?
- Could Jo have confronted Jonas differently and been successful in getting him to listen? Explain.
- Describe a time when you had to confront someone. What happened?
- Think of a time when you were confronted. What went well/poorly?
- How can you take risks successfully?
- What is the best way to handle confrontation?

# ■ Movie Title:

## *The Water Boy*

**Distributed By: Buena Vista Pictures**
**Year Created: 1998**
**MPAA rating: PG**

---

## Plot Summary:

After 18 years of being teased as a water boy by his local university
football team, Bobby Boucher is fired. Bobby is encouraged by Coach
Klein to stand up for himself and not let others walk all over him.
Despite his overprotective mother's warnings not to play, the 31-year
old Bobby secretly takes Coach Klein up on his offer and helps the
South Central Louisiana State University Mud Dogs defeat his rival
behind his mother's back.

## Description of the Scene:

Bobby answers the teacher's questions with his mother's sayings instead
of facts. The professor tells Bobby his mother is wrong. Upon hearing
the professor insult his mamma, Bobby tackles him.

**Topic Area:**                    Confrontation
                                   Feedback

**Start Time:**    **24:15**
**End Time:**    **26:15**
**Clip Duration:**    **2:00**

# Discussion Questions:

- What went wrong in this scene?
- How should Bobby have responded?
- Have you ever felt angry with the way someone responded to you? If so, what happened?
- Did the professor give Bobby feedback in an appropriate manner? What worked or didn't work?
- Is it difficult to give fair and honest feedback? Why or why not?
- How should you give feedback to a peer?
- How can you prepare someone for feedback?
- How can you receive feedback in the most productive way?

## ■ Movie Title:

# *What About Bob?*

**Distributed By: Touchstone**
**Year Created: 1991**
**MPAA rating: PG**

---

## Plot Summary:

Dr. Leo Marvin, a renowned psychiatrist, is finishing his last day of work before heading to his vacation home in New Hampshire for a month's vacation. Before closing up shop, he meets with a new patient, multi-phobic Bob. When Bob needs further help and finds Dr. Marvin gone, he follows him on vacation, befriends Marvin's family and drives Leo insane. The only way to get rid of Bob is to do it permanently.

## Description of the Scene:

Bob is having dinner with the Marvin family and absolutely loves the meal. He is over the top with appreciation to Fay (Marvin's wife) over the tasty meal.

Feedback
Motivation
Recognition

Start Time: **49:30**
End Time: **51:30**
Clip Duration: **2:00**

# Discussion Questions:

- Was Bob's appreciation sincere?
- Why is Dr. Marvin upset with Bob's accolades?
- How is Fay feeling?
- What do you do to show co-workers your appreciation?
- Have you ever received feedback that was not sincere?
  If so, how did that feel?
- What do you need to think about when giving feedback to someone?
- What are challenges with giving corrective feedback?
- Why is appreciation motivating?
- Share a time when you received positive feedback and it spurred you on.

*What About Bob?*

**Distributed By:** Touchstone
**Year Created:** 1991
**MPAA rating:** PG

## Plot Summary:

Dr. Leo Marvin, a renowned psychiatrist, is finishing his last day of work before heading to his vacation home in New Hampshire for a month's vacation. Before closing up shop, he meets with a new patient, multi-phobic Bob. When Bob needs further help and finds Dr. Marvin gone, he follows him on vacation, befriends Marvin's family and drives Leo insane. The only way to get rid of Bob is to do it permanently.

## Description of the Scene:

Dr. Marvin is fed up with Bob and has taken him into the woods where he is tying him up and placing a homemade bomb around his neck.

Analyzing Issues
Critical Thinking
Problem Solving
Stress Management

Start Time: **1:28:14**
End Time: **1:31:15**
Clip Duration: **3:01**

# Discussion Questions:

- How is Bob analyzing the situation?
- What could Dr. Marvin have done differently to solve the current situation? How did Dr. Marvin allow himself to get this extreme?
- When frustrated with someone, what do you do?
- What are the costs/benefits of taking time to make decisions?
- What are steps you can take to make the best decisions in an emotional moment?

# ■ Movie Title:

# *With Honors*

**Distributed By: Warner Brothers**
**Year Created: 1994**
**MPAA rating: PG-13**

---

## Plot Summary:

Monty is a Harvard student with a problem: his computer's hard drive crashed and he has only one copy of his thesis. On his way to make a copy of it, he accidentally drops it down a grate and into the hands of a homeless man, Simon, who is living in the basement of the library. In order to get his paper back, he must do favors for the bum. In return, he will get one page per favor.

## Description of the Scene:

Monty invites Simon to attend Professor Pitkannan's class lecture. Pitkannan is ambushing his class by asking, "What is the particular genius of the constitution? What quality distinguishes the American constitution?" Each student that has answered is "incorrect," and he belittles each. He then addresses Simon who is busy talking to Monty, and they get into a very heated debate over the Constitution.

Discrimination
Listening
Stereotypes

Start Time: **42:20**
End Time: **46:20**
Clip Duration: **4:00**

# Discussion Questions:

- What stereotypes does Pitkannan bring up about Simon?
- Is there anything discriminating about this scene? Explain.
- Is the way the professor is talking to Simon discriminating? Explain.
- What assumptions does Pitkannan make about Simon because he is a bum?
- Why did Pitkannan call on Simon in the first place?
- Have you ever been in a situation where one colleague has belittled another in public? What impact does this have on the group, if any?
- What impact (positive and negative) does stereotyping have in the workplace?
- Who does/could discrimination affect in the workplace?

## ■ Movie Title:

# *Wizard of Oz*

**Distributed By: MGM/Time Warner**
**Year Created: 1939**
**MPAA rating: G**

---

## Plot Summary:

Dorothy and her dog Toto are running away only to get caught in a storm. As she is returning home, a tornado picks her and her house up and transports her to the colorful land of Oz. When her house lands atop the Wicked Witch of the East, Dorothy is greeted with celebrity status and a warning from the Wicked Witch of the West who plans to avenge her sister's death. Dorothy and Toto travel the yellow brick road in search of a way home.

## Description of the Scene:

Dorothy is traveling down the yellow brick road with her companions when the Cowardly Lion bounds out of the forest to terrorize Dorothy and Scarecrow. When she confronts the lion and intimidates him, his real cowardice becomes apparent.

**Topic Area:** Courage
Risk Taking

**Start Time:** **49:00**
**End Time:** **51:04**
**Clip Duration:** **2:04**

# Discussion Questions:

- When you think of a lion, what qualities do you think of?
- What quality is the lion missing?
- Why is having courage important in the workplace?
- In what situations might you find you need courage at work?
- What can you do to demonstrate courage?
- Was it a risk for Dorothy to stand up to the lion?
- How can you take risks successfully?

# CHECK OUT WEBINARS WITH WOW FACTOR, ANOTHER BOOK BY BECKY PIKE PLUTH!

Death by webinar is rapidly replacing death by Power-Point! Make your webinars effective and engaging!

A webinar is a different animal—requiring different skills and a different energy—where your weaknesses and lack of preparation leave you completely exposed. Don't get caught with your training pants down!

Budget cuts and a business focus on everything "green" makes human resource training via webinars a really attractive option—IF you can do it effectively. Here is the resource you NEED for designing and delivering training that justifies your investment and gets the job done WELL.

In this book, you will discover:

- What are the top 10 sins of webinars? How can I avoid them?
- Can I connect with learners online? How?
- What are best practices for webinar design, execution and follow-up?
- What tips can I use to energize my audience?
- How can I make a powerful impact with my slide design?
- How do I use the basic webinar software tools to best advantage?
- What activities can I use to ensure participant involvement?
- What techniques can I implement to make the webinar enjoyable for both host and participant?
- How do I increase retention of the training material?

Implementing these techniques and activities are guaranteed to better prepare you to involve your participants, make your training memorable, and ensure participant action planning.

**To order copies of Webinars with WOW Factor, go to pluthconsulting.com or call 612-875-3634.**

# Index of Topics

# About the Author

A firm believer that learners will remember what they do more than what they hear, Becky has actively made her classrooms interactive with a purpose.

Becky is a training professional with more than a decade of cross-functional design and delivery impact in training, project management and business operations. A trained educator, she expanded into corporate training after completing her master's degree in teaching and learning.

With more than two decades of exposure to Bob Pike's Creative Training Techniques (CTT), she easily employs a participant-centered approach to classroom training, one-on-one training and blended e-learning. Becky infused CTT into all of her design and development while working at Target Corporation and Event Think, a multi-million dollar event management and communications company where she served Fortune 500 companies. With more than 15 years in the industry, she has designed and delivered many programs, including sessions on strategic planning, organizational-change management, sales training, train-the-trainer programs, new hire enculturation, systems training, and leadership and team development.

Becky's charismatic personality and facilitation style place participants at ease, and she empowers each learner to leave the training setting and immediately put insights into action. Sustainable, practical change and strong adult learning principles in practice are her foci. Her methods are transferable, immediately applicable and highly effective.

A partial list of her clients from The Bob Pike Group and Pluth Consulting include: Intel North America, Intel South America, NEC, Hewlett Packard, Kimberly Clark, Marshall Field's, Club Med, Target Corporation, Microsoft, Sepracor, Tampa Electric, Uline, Cisco Systems, T-Mobile, Kellogg's, and AAA.

**Invite Becky Pluth to present at your conference, training, staff development, or professional development session.** She is also available for keynotes, conference breakouts, and workshops. Call or write for more information.

Pluth Consulting, Inc.
612.875.3634
Becky.Pluth@gmail.com
www.101movieclips.com

**To purchase additional copies, or for information on bulk discounts or upcoming books by Becky Pluth, log onto www.101movieclips.com.**